CW00734134

The
Retirement
Book

by Anne Dempsey

Retirement Planning Council of Ireland September 1998

Introduction from the Chairman

Retirement as we know it today is a phenomenon of the second half of the 20th century. Men and women now retiring can look forward to a standard of living in their retirement which would have been unimaginable to all but a select few, a few generations ago.

Our Social Security systems have been developed by successive administrations and once again pensioners are looking forward to receiving real increases in the pensions paid by the Social Welfare system. At the same time, occupational pensions have developed alongside Social Welfare pensions, so that a significant proportion of our total workforce can now look forward to a reasonable standard of living in retirement.

Of course, the system is not perfect and there are still large numbers of people who do not enjoy the additional security of an occupational pension. These include the most vulnerable members of our society - the unemployed, many of the self-employed, temporary workers and those on fixed term contracts. These used to be described in Euro-speak as "atypical" workers but have become much more common in recent years because of the way in which work in our society has developed. As I write, we are considering the results of the National Pensions Policy Initiative, part of whose aims was to explore ways in which pension coverage may be extended to more and more people. The Pensions Board's recommendation that the basis Social Welfare Pensions be substantially increased and indexed in the future is most welcome.

The provision of an adequate income in retirement is not, by any means, the whole story. Financial security is just one of the pillars upon which a happy and secure retirement will be built. It is difficult to place enough emphasis on the need to prepare for the phenomenon of retirement. This preparation must encompass the whole person and must address their needs and the needs of the people around them, who will be affected to a greater or lesser extent by the impact of retirement upon the individual worker.

Some people view the prospect of retirement as a threat - others as an opportunity. Many would prefer to put off thinking about the idea until the inevitable happens. Some fear what they perceive to be a loss of status when they cease to be actively employed. Others have fears, whether well or ill founded, for their financial security, their health, or just how to fill the long hours and days which stretch before them.

The primary aim of the Retirement Planning Council of Ireland is to foster a culture among employers and workers, in which people can look forward to an active and constructive retirement. By helping to remove the fear of the unknown, we hope to assist people in enjoying a long, productive and happy retirement and we encourage employers to recognise the benefits for them in helping their workers to reap the results of the huge investment in retirement provision which they are making through occupational pension schemes.

"The Retirement Book" is a welcome addition to our toolkit. It is not designed to replace pre-retirement courses as an aid to preparing workers for retirement. Rather, we see it as a resource, a source of continuing information to which people can refer as they prepare for retirement, and in the long years of leisure that lie ahead. "The Retirement Book" is a worthy replacement for our very successful earlier book on this subject – "What Are You Doing For The Rest of Your Life?", also written by Anne Dempsey. On behalf of the Board of the Retirement Planning Council, I welcome this publication and congratulate Anne on what I believe to be a valuable addition to our bookshelves.

Paul Kenny

Chairman

Retirement Planning Council of Ireland

September 1998

Authors Acknowledgments

I would like to thank the retirement preparation course team of the Retirement Planning Council who invited me sit in on courses. Many thanks too to the many retired people who shared some of their lives. I also express my gratitude to the specialists who offered their professional expertise - Noel Beecher, Sinead Burke, Tony Collins, John Fleetwood, Brian Gallagher, Robert Grier, Mary Howe, Noel O'Sullivan, Catherine Rose and Hilary Shannon. Finally my thanks to Paul Kenny who acted as my editor.

Anne Dempsey

Contents

Chapter 1

Approaching Retirement

"Brandish your bus pass with pride ... "

*J*oe, who taught English and History, works voluntarily with the local radio since his retirement. "I manage the studio and also produce four programmes, it's a commitment of anything up to four hours a day - I enjoy it. I enjoy meeting people and the mix of young and old", he says.

"I think it's important when you wake up in the morning that there is something to do, a purpose to the day. If I did not have that, I don't think I would get up at all."

"I think the secret is to stay involved, stay physically and mentally alert and keep up with everything".

An Individual Approach

Retirement is a personal event. People bring to it differing concerns, experiences, needs and expectations. Some have given considerable thought to life after work and have a definite plan. Others don't face up to it. They didn't want to retire, didn't seek it, felt it came too soon. And even with planning, the transition can be sudden. One north Dublin businessman who retired on a Friday needed to collect something from his office the following Monday. He arrived at the car park barrier and punched in his identity card. Entry was refused. Already he had been automatically written out of the system. Similarly a busy G.P. talks about the phone going strangely silent the week after he retired. 'I wondered was it broken', he said.

Planning

But planning will help. You will be psychologically prepared to some degree if you look at your life-style now and envisage how it transfers into retirement. People tend to get out of retirement what they put into it. What do you most want to happen? Plan to make it happen. What do you least want to happen? Plan to prevent it happening. If you want a fulfiling retirement, it will help to plan for it.

The people who long for an end to work and see retirement with rose-tinted spectacles may be unrealistic. Retirement won't be all sweetness and light. At a midway stage in life, most people know that life has joys and sorrows. This won't change. Retirement is about options.

When it comes to planning, research has shown that the further away from retirement you start to plan the better. However, so called abstracts such as pension, tax, lump sum and leisure become more concrete when retirement is round the corner.

A sampling of attitudes among a group facing retirement illustrates the many individual approaches to it. Some looked forward to it, and felt they would enjoy more leisure and freedom together. One couple planned to move to the Canaries, rent their house in Ireland and so have continued income from it. A widower with a son living abroad plans to visit him more frequently. Back in Ireland, he does voluntary work and hopes to expand this area of interest.

Others had a less hopeful approach. A single woman living alone knows she will miss the social aspect of work. She realises she will need to make more local contacts if she is not to be rather solitary in retirement.

Others worried that they would miss the cut and thrust from work. People spoke about the sense of impending loss of job, status, organisation, friends, satisfaction and achievement they associated with work. Some felt rejected, said they were at their peak in terms of experience but were no longer wanted, and that hurt. Some talked about missing the discipline of routine, the reason to get up in the morning. Still more said the nature of work had changed, there was too much pressure and they would be glad to leave the fast lane for the quieter margins.

The Gift of Time

Despite the personal nature of retirement, there are common strands all retired people share. One is the gift of time that lands quite suddenly in your lap. You can underestimate the amount of time you spend at work. If you have worked an eight hour day all your life, you would have worked about 2,400 hours per year. Over a 40 year working life, that's about 100,000 hours.

It is a lot of time. Ideally the hours spilling into your life should be regarded not only as a gift but as something earned, part of the job package that includes wages, holidays, sick benefit and pension. The work ethic, so strongly ingrained, can cause some people to feel guilty when they stop conventional work. But retirement is a new time of opportunity and entitlement.

Ageing

Retirement is often associated with the negative aspects of ageing. "I don't consider myself old" said one man on a retirement course recently. "My heart feels about 30." He was speaking for many. We usually see ourselves as chronologically younger than we are.

And if retirement is often linked with growing old, being old is often stereotyped as being dependent, poor, bedridden, senile, feeble. Some people may fear that age 65, the age of mandatory retirement for many, is when they start to get old.

There is no particular age at which you get old. While many 70, 80 even 90 year olds are still full of life, there are 40 year olds who have become set in their ways. Age effect is influenced by attitude. Years ago when people retired at 65 they were in their twilight years. This is no longer the case. Chronological age is just a date on a calendar. Much more interesting is biological ageing. If you can combine mental and physical health, you can forget about chronological ageing. This means thinking positively.

However, there are negative connotations still attached to old age in Ireland today, and many of the ageist views are promoted often unconsciously, by middle-aged people themselves. A pre-retirement group was recently asked to estimate what percentage of the over-65s are being looked after in nursing homes. The group felt that three in every four 65 year olds is so dependent. In fact, according to a recent health survey, only 5%, (or one in 20) of 65s and over are in residential care. 78% – almost four in every five – live at home with some or no support. Frequently it's the perceptions about being older that need to be challenged, rather than the reality.

Age Stereotyping

As well as categorising people by age, we also attribute negative qualities to older people. One of the dangers of retirement is that well-meaning people will begin to see you as old, and act accordingly. They may question your ability to make decisions.

Don't let other people's perceptions, however caring, limit and affect your life. Don't subscribe to the negative. Growing older is something to celebrate. You have the wisdom of experience. You may be wiser, more reflective, happier and more at peace with yourself than you were thirty years ago. It's up to you to challenge an inaccurate stereotype. You can be a positive role model. Some older people seem to be ashamed of being older.

You see them, for example, furtively showing their bus pass as if ashamed of their years. Don't add to ageist attitudes by subscribing to them yourself. Brandish that bus pass with pride. You've earned it! ·

Early Retirement

While the most common retirement age is 65 for both men and women, many people are now retiring early, some as early as 50. This is happening both in the public and private sector across a range of jobs from semiskilled to management. The reasons are both industry- and consumer-led. Companies wanting to trim the payroll are offering attractive early retirement packages to executives at the top of their earnings curve. Company costs in funding a retirement package from pension funds can be more easily borne than funding top level salaries for the foreseeable future. Also people are interested in retiring early - part of a general change in attitude towards work and the place it holds in our lives.

Early retirement has attractions. It gives options, a chance to try something new. Early in your life you had to make choices which meant closing some doors. Retirement offers an opportunity to open those doors again, and the more years of active retirement you have, the more you can do.

There is a danger, however, in leaving employment abruptly without thinking through the implications of the move. Consider the changes involved. Work gives life a structure and a status. People who retire at 65 move into a different category which can have its own status. Those who retire early may have difficulty finding their niche, there can be neighbourhood mutterings 'it's well for some' if you're around during the day. You may need a good self image to counter this.

And even the most attractive package has to be looked at critically as it will have to last for longer. An early retirement lump sum must be invested prudently, hedging as much as possible against changing financial times. A climate of low inflation and high interest rates is normally good for retirees, but the opposite - high inflation and low interest - can erode a nest egg quite briskly over the years.

You may find you have retired at a time when other changes are happening within your family - such as children studying for exams, or leaving home. The family too needs to be prepared for your change in employment and status.

Redundancy

Some leave-takings from work are involuntary and unwelcome. Every year about 20,000 people are made redundant. The shift to jobs in the service sector, the growth in part-time work and the need or wish of many employers to rationalise has led to reduced employment of older workers. Also the availability of a large pool of qualified young people with technological literacy has led to companies letting older workers go early and hiring young people at lower costs. Redundancy can cause feelings of rejection much stronger than those engendered by retirement. Many made redundant need to be particularly prudent with severance pay. So you may have many questions as you contemplate life after work – whether in the immediate or more distant future, whether through retirement at 65, early retirement or redundancy. Will my pension be enough to see me through? Will I have to take a drop in my standard of living? How will I best invest my lump sum? How will my tax situation be affected when I retire? Will I be bored? Will time hang heavily? As a single person, I get on well with the people I work with, will I miss what they offer? As a married person, how will I cope with all this togetherness? Read on.

Chapter 2

Coping with change

"Trying to live in the past"

Fame came late to Alice. She was in her fifties when her first book appeared, heralding a new fully-fledged talent on the Irish literary scene. More books followed, leading to recognition at home and abroad.

"I think because all this has come to me later in life, I can cope with it", she says. "I wouldn't have learned very much if I hadn't learned that fame is fickle, and that the private, local aspect of my life is still crucially important: walking with my friends, walking in the woods, my prayer group.

"I don't feel old, I feel I have matured, with a better appreciation of life now. This is a very rich time, a kind of late blossoming".

Lifelong Change

About 30,000 people reach retirement age in Ireland every year, and the majority of those in the workforce retire at age 65. Even if you've been looking forward to it, retirement may represent some sense of loss - and change. Probably one of the biggest life changes after joining the workforce is leaving it. However, to be human means to be able to change, most people learn to cope with change as they go through life. People retiring today have already mastered huge social changes - and the older you are, the more changes you have faced. Some people in their 90's today were born before the launch of the motor car, and now we have walked on the moon. Thirty years ago many Irish homes had no telephone. Today many homes are not only computerised but are linked to the Internet. Such is the pace of twentieth century technological evolution.

As a middle-aged person, you have already dealt with many life adjustments. You might like to tick off the following changes big and small you have already experienced:

- leaving home for that first day at school

- success and or failure in examinations

- leaving school and getting a job

- migration from your own town or emigration to another country

- being promoted or demoted

- losing a job

- unemployment

- redundancy

- marriage

- separation

- having and rearing children

- seeing them leaving home

- becoming a grandparent

- illness

- accidents

- bereavement

Many people nearing retirement will have experienced some of these and coped – without necessarily ever having done a course in managing change.

Life Stages

The philosopher Erik Erikson looks at ageing from a psychological point of view, and divides our lives into chapters and stages. He maintains that understanding people in later life needs a more long term view: "One must see them in the context of their whole life history with the problems both successfully and unsuccessfully resolved from earlier periods", he says.

The key element in understanding his theories includes a life framework in which different tasks are to be done at different stages. These stages and tasks include:

• early adulthood for the development of intimacy

• middle age to establish and guide the next generation

• old age to attain age integrity, a sense of meaning and order in life.

He further believes that personal circumstances change and vary according to life history so, the longer you live, the more diverse and individual you become.

What Work Gives - Positive

In order to look at the transition from work to retirement it may be important to identify the factors which work offers so that these can be compensated for, if possible. So what does the job mean to you? What qualities does work give?

Work gives status. Rightly or wrongly, people tend to make judgements and assessments about you, based on the career path you chose.

Work gives identity. The more closely you identify with the job and the more it spills into your life, the greater the problem there may be when the job is no more. Many doctors, academics, military personnel keep the job title when they retire, an indication, perhaps, that who they feel they are is inextricably tied up with what they do. At a course for redundant management personnel, it emerged that some hadn't told their families they had no job until the PRSI ran out – their identity was so fused with their job that they couldn't admit it had gone.

Work means income, allowing you to be independent, set up your own home, perhaps to marry and have a family.

Work means training, skills acquisition, learning, excitement, challenge, variety, self-esteem, mental stimulation, and the comfort of habit.

Ideally work has helped you meet human needs both basic and complex. These are often referred to as a hierarchy of needs, first chronicled by the American psychologist, Abraham Maslow. and sometimes shown graphically as a pyramid, with needs listed in order of descending priority.

At the bottom are your basic physical needs – for survival, food, shelter, rest. Next comes your need for security. This is defined as safety, predictability, routine, income. Third up is social and tribal – association, friendship, group belonging.

Near the top is self esteem – confidence, status, recognition. At the top of the list is self realisation, which Maslow defines as using your talents and will for fulfilment. His concepts have been accepted as a crucial tenet of human motivation.

What Work Gives - Negative

Work can also mean hassle, stress, anxiety, bullying, inconvenience, injustice, fatigue, harassment, rush and fuss, disappointment, worry and boredom.

The negative aspects of work can grow over the years. Also when you spend years in one company, the challenge it offered can be eroded. The job at 60 may not be providing the level of satisfaction and self-esteem that it did at 40.

This may be due in part to new procedures, new management, new technology, new younger colleagues. Can I cope? Your security and self-esteem may be eroded. A younger person may seem to do it so much better. So in completing the equation about what work gives, it's good to be honest and say exactly how it is now, rather than fooling yourself.

It could be helpful at this stage to do a personal stock-taking:

- Where am I in life?
- What have I achieved
- What is still to achieve?
- Is it feasible?
- If yes, how can I achieve it?
- Could I afford to retire?
- What would I do in retirement?
- What are my skills, talents, interests?
- How can I achieve personal satisfaction if this is not given through my job?

Changes When You Leave

So what will change when you leave work? Answer - almost everything. Your daily base, routine, style of life, relationships will change. Your stress levels and your boredom threshold may be altered, as will your status, real or perceived. It's important to look at what is going on emotionally after the farewell party, the presentations, the back slapping and citations. When the lights go out and silence descends, how is retirement personally to be faced?

Experiencing Change

People may say they're not going to allow events to change their life. But everything that happens to you changes you. Change is a process, and how you handle it will determine the outcome to a large extent.

Change is sometimes represented graphically as a time of turbulence between two poles of stability.

While life before and after change may be depicted as stable, with each state different from the other, the wavy lines linking the two states illustrate the process involved in moving from one to the other. People who manage the process successfully have coped with change.

Change is a one way street. Invariably you must go forward. Behind there is a 'no entry' sign. If you don't like the change, if you don't want to go forward, you will be stuck in a kind of limbo. You can't enjoy the present, you keep trying to live in the past. This can be evident in the way some retired people hark back to their jobs, wondering why they were let go, convinced that nobody can do the work as well as they. It may be true, but moving on inevitably means letting go some of the past.

Because change is often difficult, it can engender strong and powerful feelings. These can run the gamut from anger – 'who the hell are they to fire me?' to depression – 'if I'd been better they might have kept me on, I'm no good'.

The steps which some people experience while undergoing change include:

1. SHOCK: this may be pleasant or unpleasant. You may be delighted if asked to attend a pre-retirement course. Or you may be very taken aback.

2. EUPHORIA: arises from an unwillingness to face reality, to deny what has happened. It generally doesn't last too long before reality comes crashing in.

3. DENIAL: You may feel events are moving too quickly. You might want to deny the reality. 'I'm not really retired, I'll think about it after the Christmas holidays',

4. SELF DOUBT: You begin to feel in a vacuum. Life no longer has its familiar structure or purpose. You may begin to question your identity and worth. You are no longer a garda or bank clerk, shop assistant or brain surgeon. So who are you?

5. TESTING: You begin to test your new life. Often unconsciously, you experiment with new roles, behaviours, activities, ideas, even with the way you dress. This can be a time of trial and error as you take up something and find you hate it, move on to something else and realise you enjoy it. The strength of this time is its fluidity. This is the beginning of the transition to the final phase.

6. ACCEPTANCE: One day you wake up and realise you are in a new place psychologically. You have accepted that you are retired. Your life is different, it incorporates a somewhat altered philosophy, ideally based on realistic assessment of past, present and future.

There is no standard timescale for the completion of the steps involved in change at retirement. They could take weeks or months, but generally shouldn't take more than a year. It is also worth bearing in mind that change affects different people in different ways. You may not necessarily experience any or all of the stages outlined. Equally, you may experience some of the feelings outlined above, without being consciously aware of what you are going through.

Looking at change from a slightly different perspective, psychologists identify four stages in negotiating retirement – completing the stages means embracing each.

FACE: The first stage is about facing the reality of what has happened. This can be difficult at first. You may be physically at home, but emotionally still at work. You may have feelings of confusion and displacement.

EXPRESS: The second stage of letting go is to express your feelings. These could be of sadness and/or anger as well as uncertainty, depression, fear, grief. Some people, because of their background or past experience of loss, can get stuck at a particular stage and find it difficult to move on. They want to stay in touch with the job, continue to 'phone and drop in. Unfortunately, they may be in the way, see unfamiliar, younger faces which can reinforce feelings of rejection and hurt.

ACCEPT: The third stage of letting go is an acknowledgement that new life is possible. This could be as simple as deciding to walk to the local shop for the morning paper just to see whom you will meet. At a subconscious level this may be signalling the need for social contacts, the acceptance that these can be found locally and an affirmation of their value.

EMBRACE: The fourth and final stage of letting go is opening up to your new life. This will probably mean some new activities, new friends. There is an internal shift, an acceptance that, while life has changed, there are possibilities for enjoyment and challenge in the future as there were in the past.

You can't skip a stage. Some people don't want to let go of the past because they fear that would mean forgetting it and somehow invalidating it. But letting go doesn't mean forgetting. When you come through the four stages, you find that you don't have to forget the past, that somehow you have integrated it with your present. The past has become part of you. You are no longer working in a particular profession, but you are still the same person with the same talents, ideas, vision. You reclaim yourself.

Life in Retirement

A different discipline and the granting of freedom is the most obvious change in retirement. Freedom is positive, but it can be a tyranny too. Some people feel very jittery when they come out of hospital or prison - or anywhere where their days have been heavily structured and there has been comparatively little freedom. Your place of work may not have been a prison, but it has offered a structure, which is now missing. You have a lot of freedom suddenly. You may thrive on it, and feel spontaneous for the first time in ages. Or you may begin to feel uneasy, purposeless.

If you are the kind of person who likes a structure, you may need to impose your own routine in retirement. 'Wednesday is library day', 'I'll walk the dog every evening at nine o'clock', and so on.

On the other hand, if you've waited 40 years to be rid of routine, that's okay too. It's important to know what kind of person you are, what will give you fulfilment, because your successful retirement will be unique to you and will depend on your wishes, your circumstances, your income, health, and life- style.

Bearing in mind that your hierarchy of needs won't change in retirement, it could be helpful to look at Maslow's pyramid to see how you can create opportunities to continue to have these needs met - particularly in the three higher areas, social association, self-esteem and self-realisation. You will find other chapters offering ideas on this.

A Retirement Preparation Course?

A retirement preparation course gives you the opportunity to reflect before you retire. You can look at the areas of your life that will change, such as: routine, time, status, income, relationships, health, leisure. A course enables you to make the decisions about your life that only you can make. No one else can make these decisions for you.

Many people find that a retirement preparation course can be helpful in clarifying their concerns regarding leaving work, and helping them understand the kind of emotional and practical changes they will face. A retirement preparation course can:

- give you the space and opportunity to stop and take stock
- help to engender a positive attitude to life after retirement
- give you a framework for identifying short- and more long-term priorities in line with your personal objectives

- offer relevant information, and point you in the right direction to find out more

- provide an opportunity to explore feelings and attitudes towards retirement, with spouse or significant other

- give the chance to name, face and consider solutions for particular fears and problems.

A word to employers

While fewer than 10% of the Irish workforce has traditionally been offered a retirement preparation course by their employer, that is changing. Today more employers, trade unions and individuals are coming to see the benefits and value of early preparation for retirement. From the employer's point of view, a retirement course can:

- give reassurance and a sense of direction to older employees, and so improves general morale

- increase employee's knowledge and appreciation of the company pension and lump sum options and may, therefore, take some of the workload from personnel staff and pension trustees

- facilitate the transition to retirement and so preserve a good working environment for all staff

- reduce the need for employee counselling

  assist in more effective manpower planning

- create good relations with retired staff, keeping the door open for short-term re-engagement or consultancy if needed

- improve company image as a caring employer, both inside the organisation and in the wider community.

Retirement preparation in Ireland

The Retirement Planning Council of Ireland, (RPCI) runs two-day retirement planning courses throughout Ireland. In house courses are available tailored for a particular company or organisation. Open courses will have individuals from a cross-section of companies represented.

Each participant is encouraged to bring another family member who will be affected by the retirement – spouse, parent, brother, sister, son, daughter, or a friend. Courses cover the following topics:

- change and coping with change

- attitudes to work

- financial issues, such as investments, savings, taxation, and – social welfare entitlements

- legal matters, specifically wills,

- home safety and security

- pension entitlements, and

- healthy living

For more information regarding any aspect of retirement or retirement preparation, contact the *Retirement Planning Council of Ireland, Retirement Consultants, 27/29 Pembroke Street Lower, Dublin 2, Tel 01-6613139.*

Chapter 3

Friends, Family and Relationships

"Retirement will bring a lot more togetherness ..."

*M*oira, an actress, was a leading character in a television series which was Ireland's first rural soap opera. The series ran from 1965 to 1978, and was part catalyst, part reflection of our transition from a rural sheltered island into a modern cosmopolitan nation.

"I am different from the part I played," says Moira, "I like a drink and a smoke - she touched neither. She was a worrier, a bit of a goody-goody, no bit of craic about her as I think I have".

The Significant Others

More than a third of Irish households are made up of extended family with different generations living together. When you retire, the people close to you are affected also. In retirement, your relationships with family, neighbours and friends can become even more important, whether you are married, widowed, single, and whether you live alone, or with a friend or are one of a couple. If you're single, work may have offered a significant social outlet. If you're married, leaving work brings opportunities - and challenges.

The Gift of Time

On retirement you get a gift of perhaps 2,500 hours a year which sounds wonderful. But surveys show that perhaps 80% of your social circle tends to be work-related, and the day you leave, these are the people to whom you say goodbye. So you may have plenty of time, but nobody ready to fill it with. You need to look at ways in which to reconstitute the 80%, and so add to your existing circle of friends and acquaintances. You may have to get out and make contacts. Don't cut yourself off, we're not meant to be too alone.

Retirement Concerns

For people who live in a relationship with parent, brother, sister, retirement will bring a lot more togetherness than before. For partners/spouses, retirement has been described as a kind of second marriage, giving more hours in each other's company than perhaps since the early days of marriage.

Many married couples, no matter how devoted, may be a bit apprehensive about retirement. This is very natural, an indication of mutual awareness that things are different. Talking things over will help, and this is one of the values of doing a retirement preparation course together. When encouraged to share their feelings, some men wonder if they should keep out of their wife's way for part of the day. Some women are concerned that his being at home all day will adversely affect her freedom.

Alternatively, a man may have retired while a wife, sister or partner continues to work. This involves getting used to a new routine - which will change again when she retires. Research shows that many relationships experience some turbulence during the early stages of retirement. But these life changes usually need only a bit of mutual give and take, and after an initial adjustment, most couples settle happily into a satisfying and enjoyable retirement.

A minority of couples may have deeper issues. Unfulfilled parts of a marriage can be masked by work and busy leisure. After retirement these issues may be impossible to evade. Work can be a shock absorber when things go wrong at home. When this is removed, problems which had been suppressed, may emerge.

Some time ago a group of women who work full-time at home came together to discuss their husbands' retirement. The first few waxed lyrical about their future new life. They were looking forward to being together, couldn't wait. A fifth woman stopped everyone short by saying she dreaded the day. She explained that she was married to a control freak. Weekends were already difficult, how would it be when he was there all the time?

Her honesty brought everyone on to a more even keel. What's it going to be like for me? How will my routine alter? I'm used to going into town, popping in next door, will this change? How about finances? What about our life-style, cars, holidays, outings? Will I get half the money but twice the hassle? These were some of the questions asked.

A Family Affair

So the tasks involved in moving into retirement have implications for the role of the significant others in your life. Ideally, if you are close to your partner, and used to talking things out together, retirement is another issue you will face jointly. Remember too that while you're the one retiring, your partner may be experiencing problems also. For example, a certain kind of wife invests heavily in her husband's career. There is the story of the woman by the river bank shouting 'Help, help, my husband the civil engineer is drowning!' When he retires, she can have difficulty in coming to terms with the change in status and identity involved.

There are implications too for children, and relatives, who may not have the patience or empathy to understand if you're feeling low. They just may not want to hear. Or well-meaning people can leap in with advice, 'I think you ought to do this, or this', when all you need to do at this point is to take your time and reflect on what's going on.

Getting Routines in Harmony

Your retirement may throw into sharp relief the differing routines in your home. For years you will have had your own routine, typically getting up early, leaving for work, your day punctuated by midmorning, lunch and afternoon breaks, arriving back home between 6-8pm. Or you may have been a night worker, or been on shift work - whatever your pattern, there will have been a predictable routine built up over the years.

But your spouse, parent, sister or partner, whether working inside or outside the home will have had her/his own routine, as will your children. Each routine may be relatively unknown to the other. Typically the home-based spouse has a model with a series of blocks of work and relaxation throughout the day. The routine has been flexible. They have probably been their own boss for many years. The two routines may have little in common, and have had different starting and finishing points.

Once one of the couple retires, finding new complementary routines is very important. This new pattern may fall into place naturally, or it may need a bit of help. One way is for both of you to separately make out a 'wish list' of what you would like to do in retirement. Swap lists, go through them, and agree some of the common points.

There may be rows if you avoid sorting out this issue of how you spend your time, or begin imposing routines on each other. If a wife has a list of jobs for the newly retired husband, he may feel he has exchanged one jailer for another. Or the retired man can become the boss. He can begin to question: 'where are you going, you went there yesterday'? 'Are you going to buy that or not?' 'When will you be back?' Not surprisingly, such questions will be resented. Retirement gives you back your personal space. But it doesn't give you the right to impose your new freedom on someone else.

Marriage/Partnership

How can married love be kept alive over the decades? One psychologist specialising in relationship issues offers the following suggestions.

- Retain some of the rules of courtship. Perhaps Wednesday was always the night you spent time together. Stick to that principle. Take time for yourselves.

- Keep in touch emotionally. Find out how each of you is feeling. Try to tell the truth to each other, otherwise things will mount up. So when you talk, really try to tune in.

- Show your appreciation. Surprise with little gestures – the bunch of flowers, the surprise book or gift. Little things still mean a lot.

- Practise real listening. The key element of good communication is listening, treating each other with respect. A good way to listen is to reflect back, ask questions about what is said, clarify what you don't understand.

- Assert yourself if necessary. Good relationships are founded on justice and mutual respect.

- Keep in touch sexually. Don't compare yourselves to other couples. Do what pleases you both. The only marriage you can know from the inside out is your own.

- Accept that the empty nest left when grown up children leave home can impose new pressures as well as new freedoms.

- Don't expect perfection. There's no such thing as a perfect couple. If you find yourself being irritated by petty faults in the other, make a list of all the positive things about them.

- Don't live in each other's pockets. Have a mix of friends including his friends, her friends and common friends you see together.

- Laugh together as much as possible.

- Get help if needed sooner rather than later. Sometimes marriage counselling is seen as a last resort. In planning for retirement, if you're experiencing marriage problems, take action now, rather than waiting.

Adult Children

Over time we go through many aspects of change and loss - loss of youth, parents, friends emigrating. For parents there may be the loss of children growing up and going away. It's tough. But good parenting involves having the courage to let your growing children think for themselves, speak for themselves, even make a fool of themselves - in safety - if necessary. The letting go never stops from kindergarten to college and beyond. Nothing is harder for a parent to do - or more necessary.

Present a united front with grown up children. Often a mother may have become the emotional broker, caring too much. In retirement, a father may take time to find a new relationship with adult children and grandchildren.

Grandparents

The very young and older people have a lot in common. As grandparents you can provide a sense of family history and roots by talking about the old days. Many children lose out through lack of grandparental contact. Also, some grandparents are good at breaking through the generation gap and can talk to grandchildren on subjects difficult to discuss with their parents. Equally grandchildren may give you a sense of continuation, affirming your link with creating future generations, as well as a chance to enjoy the wonder and company of young people to whom you are intimately connected.

Chapter 4

Healthy and Happy

"… Routine maintenance"

" People try to put me down because of my age, but I won't have it" says
*Grace. "The feeling you often get is 'she's old, anything is good enough for
her'. I challenge them on it, politely but firmly, I don't put up with it."*

*In her eighties, Grace has an extended family of children, grandchildren and great
grandchildren. "The family is very important, I keep up with them all. Also, I'm
greedy, greedy for learning, for life. I've lived through so much, that I think it gives a
wisdom. You are able to take a long-term view. One of the benefits of being old is
that you can get away with anything. You're forgiven".*

Introduction

Growing older doesn't mean growing less healthy, and most people in
their fifties, sixties and beyond remain well and fit. Perhaps you can't sprint
for the bus the way you used to thirty years ago, but maybe you get up on
time these days anyway, so avoiding the need for a last minute rush. Fitness
is correctly defined not as the ability to run a four minute mile, but
generally having the energy and puff to live the life you want.

Keeping well in retirement involves taking care of your physical,
emotional and psychological health – and this obviously has implications for
life-style now and later.

Physical Health

So a good idea before retirement or around the time you retire is to have
a health check, ideally from a GP who knows you and your family history.
It will include an examination of your weight, heart, blood pressure, lungs,
abdomen, teeth, a check for any sores, urine check for the presence of
diabetes, chest Xray, ECG, and blood tests. As you get older, regular eye,
dental and chiropody checks are important too.

Men's Health Issues

As a man you have an lower life expectancy than women. So what makes
the male so vulnerable?

The answer may be attitude. Many men don't look after their health.
There is a prevailing attitude 'if it ain't broke, don't fix it' which leads to lack
of routine maintenance, a reluctance to go for a physical check up and

regular service. This lack of commitment to preventative measures is a passport to poor health. In a recent health survey four out of five men admit to leaving problems too long before going for medical advice, and only one in ten would consider visiting the GP for a preventative check up.

Neglecting an area of our health may seem to have no immediate consequences. However, poor habits laid down earlier in life can begin to bite as we grow older, also some parts of the body do begin to wear out with the passing of the years.

In this chapter, we look at the kind of ailments which can emerge with advancing years, and at some strategies to help yourself to better health. See also *Chapter 5 Fit and Well.*

Male Cancers

About 6,500 men are diagnosed with cancer each year, with skin and lung cancer leading the field. Approximately 1,400 Irish men every year find they have skin cancer, while about 1,120 are treated for lung cancer. The three other most common cancers in men in order of incidence are bowel, prostate, and lip cancer. If you experience any of the warning signs described below, do consult your doctor. Many of today's cancers can be cured if caught on time.

Skin Cancer

The causes are prolonged or repeated exposure to sunlight or ultra-violet irradiation. Depending on your type of work, you should be aware of exposure to arsenic, oils, tar, pitch and other chemicals. Warning signs are dry, scaly patches, or skin sores or ulcers that don't heal, warts or moles which change in size or appearance, unusual lumps on your skin.

Reduce your risk factors by avoiding excessive exposure to sun or ultra violet lamps. Clean your skin thoroughly if using chemical substances, wear protective clothing and follow recommended procedures. If working or relaxing in the open, cover up. Wear a hat with a brim. Wear a Tshirt on a hot day, and a sunblock with a high sun protection factor (SPF).

Lung Cancer

Cigarette smoking has been established as the main risk factor for lung cancer. Warning signs are persistent cough, difficulty in breathing, chest pain or coughing up blood. If you don't smoke, don't start. If you do smoke, consider cutting down, or better still, cutting out.

Bowel Cancer

Cancer of the bowel (colon and rectum) is linked to diet and is highest in western countries where people eat over refined foods. The warning signs are changes in bowel habits which may include constipation, recurring diarrhoea. Blood in the bowel motions may signal bowel trouble including cancer, but this is a screening test only. To guard against bowel cancer, eat plenty of wholemeal bread, cereals with fibre, fibrous vegetables such as potatoes, parsnips, turnips and baked beans, and fruit.

Prostate Cancer

The prostate - part muscle, part gland - is situated at the neck of the bladder. Prostate cancer is age-related and problems are most common in older men. Warning signs are connected with urinating, and include pain and difficulty, frequency, and blood in the urine.

Lip Cancer

Lip cancer has been linked to smoking, heavy drinking and poor dental hygiene. Warning signs are sore or cracked lips which don't heal, puckering or thickening of skin on the lip. Again prevention is to avoid smoking, don't drink too much, visit your dentist regularly, take corrective action if your dentures don't fit properly and brush your teeth regularly.

Testicular Cancer

Today there is a 95-100% cure rate for testicular cancer which occurs most usually in young and middle-aged men. Regularly examine each testicle for lumps. See your doctor right away if you notice either a firm painless swelling, or experience pain and inflammation in either.

The following are the guidelines for reducing your risk factors for all types of cancer:

1. Don't smoke.
2. Drink less alcohol.
3. Avoid unprotected sun exposure.
4. Follow work safety regulations regarding production and handling of cancer-causing substances.
5. Eat fresh fruits, vegetables and high-fibre cereals.
6. Keep slim, lose excess weight gradually by eating less fatty foods and taking regular exercise.

7. See a doctor if you notice a lump, a change in a mole or have abnormal bleeding.

8. See a doctor for a persistent cough, hoarseness, change in bowel habits or unexplained weight loss.

Heart Disease

While heart disease is on the increase among the female population, men are still more prone to it than are women. They say the way to a man's heart is through his stomach, which can be tragically true. Many men develop heart disease through a too-fatty diet, particularly so in Ireland where we liberally butter our spuds, drink gallons of full cream milk and may fry rather than grill food.

One in three Irish deaths is from heart disease and while the figures have dropped in America, Australia and some parts of Europe, Ireland still has the dubious honour of staying near the top of heart disease table.

There is no secret of the causes of heart disease. The ten villains are: high blood fats, smoking, high blood pressure, overweight, eating too much fatty salty foods, taking too little exercise, a family history of coronary heart disease, stress. And – significantly – being male.

There are different types of heart disease. Angina pectoris means chest pain or tightness, caused perhaps by the stress of unaccustomed exercise. This is due to a narrowing or silting up of the arteries which restricts the flow of blood, and the pain is a type of heart cramp.

Treatment can include surgery (which short circuits the affected arteries with new blood vessels), drugs, elimination of risk factors to avoid a recurrence, and some change of life-style.

Thrombosis means blood clot and a coronary thrombosis is a heart attack caused by clot or blockage of an artery which cuts off blood supply to a part of the heart muscle. The symptom is chest pain which can strike suddenly, and spread across chest, arms, neck and jaw. The greatest treatment advance these days is the coronary care unit. Any complications are identified and treated immediately. If necessary, a clot-dissolving injection can help reverse the effects of the attack.

Lowering Your Risk of Heart Disease

1. Don't smoke

If you want to stop smoking, plan. Work out to 'Q' (quit) day. Start by putting back the time of day at which you have the first smoke. Gradually make it later and later. Plan not to smoke in certain places. Cut down on the actual number of cigarettes you smoke each day.

2. Have your blood pressure and blood cholesterol level checked

If too high, take action. Weight loss, reduced alcohol intake, physical activity and low fat, low salt diet will help reduce blood and cholesterol levels.

3. Eat a balanced diet

Choose a variety of foods. Eat plenty of fruit, vegetables, fish and chicken. Choose lean meat and avoid frying or adding fat when cooking. Eat wholegrain bread and cereals, and eat potatoes without added fat.

4. Watch your alcohol intake, and if necessary reduce

5. Lose weight gradually if overweight

Aim to lose one or two pounds a week. Gradual weight loss which involves building up healthier eating habits will be much more effective than dramatic crash diets.

6. Take regular exercise

Choose a type of exercise that suits your life-style. Make realistic plans to fit activity into your daily schedule. If after a month's trial you are not making progress and not enjoying it, think again. Maybe it would help to walk with a friend, to change the time of day you set aside for exercise, or to try some other type of activity.

7. See a doctor if you experience chest or leg pains

These can be an indicator of arterial disease.

Prostate

Prostate trouble will affect about one in ten men over the age of 60. The prostate gland surrounds the urethra - the tube which passes urine from the bladder to the penis. As you get older, the gland may enlarge, which can affect the ease with which you can pass water. The flow of urine may be choked, or emptying the bladder may be painful, or there may be dribbling of urine. Treatment may involve an operation to remove the prostate, in whole or in part, and so relieve the problem.

Some men with prostate problems suffer in silence rather than going to their doctor. The embarrassment may be helped by knowing that such problems are common and relatively straightforward to deal with.

Male Impotence

Male impotence is the inability to achieve an erection adequate for successful sexual intercourse. Impotence can be temporary, caused by stress or tiredness. The more permanent cases of impotence may be due to diabetes, hardening of the arteries, high cholesterol levels, bladder or prostate problems.

Mid-life Crisis

Feeling tired, depressed, lacking direction? You are not alone. More than one out of every two men questioned in a recent poll believed they had been through a midlife crisis between 40 - 60. The symptoms included aches and pains, feelings of doubt about the value of their lives so far and uncertainty about the future. Some men become depressed and irritable, feel tired, lack concentration. A number complain of losing their sex drive.

One psychotherapist working with such men explains what's going on: "Many men spend their young adult years working hard, building up careers, raising a family, meeting goals. Suddenly, they see retirement or redundancy ahead, they wonder what it's all been about".

Some of the reasons are physical and due to lowering testosterone levels. Boosting the male hormone level can slow down the ageing process and give men back their zest for life. Hormone replacement therapy for men is now becoming available. But for most men, talking things over with someone, perhaps a GP, or counsellor, can be a great help.

Men will also be helped by caring families and friends who allow them express their feelings. "Midlife is an important life stage" says philosopher Erik Erikson, "it is a time when nature pushes men to make the final transition from youth to maturity, a way of forcing them to go forward"

Women's Health Issues

Women live longer than men. This may be partly because they look after their physical health needs better than do men, and approach emotional problems in a way which allows them receive more support from family and friends, and so perhaps lowering stress levels. However, it is also being found that as women take on more traditional male roles i.e. working full time outside the home, they are becoming more susceptible to so-called male diseases such as heart disease. These days cancers and heart disease are a major threat to women's health.

Female Cancers

Breast cancer is the most common type of cancer among women, though women who smoke will also be in danger from contracting lung cancer. Skin cancer is also on the increase among women as well as men and some women may be at risk of contracting cervical cancer. The guidelines given above to lower cancer risk factors equally apply to women.

Breast cancer

The three most important points to know about breast cancer are that most lumps are benign, that many breast cancers are curable and that the sooner you go to your doctor if you notice a change in your breasts, the better.

One in 12 has a chance of developing breast cancer. Symptoms could be a lump usually painless, an inverted nipple, swelling in breast or armpits, a puckered or dimpled breast.

Possible risk factors include a family history of breast cancer, early puberty, late menopause, being overweight, and a too fatty diet.

If the lump is malignant it will be removed (lumpectomy), or the breast will be removed (mastectomy). Radio or chemotherapy may be used also. If the tumour is small and detected early, a complete cure is likely. Losing your breast can be traumatic, family support and understanding helps a lot. Most women would say losing a breast is preferable to losing a life.

Lower your risk of breast cancer by avoiding too much animal protein, saturated animal fat and dairy produce. Examine your breasts thoroughly each month. Many doctors recommend that women aged over 50, have a regular mammogram, (breast Xray), though not every doctor recommends this as a form of health screening.

Cervical cancer

Cervical cancer, or cancer of the neck of the womb, can be detected in a pre-cancerous stage and is completely curable if caught in time through regular smear tests.

Principally a disease of sexually active women, it is the second commonest female cancer, particularly in women under 35. Possible risk factors include multiple sexual partners and smoking. However, it is not confined exclusively to younger women, and older women too can contract cervical cancer. Symptoms include irregular vaginal bleeding between periods or after sex. Treatment is a combination of surgery, radiotherapy and chemotherapy. There is a 75% survival rate if no recurrence surfaces five years after treatment.

A cervical smear test every few years has proved to be an effective way of detecting the very early signs of cancerous and pre-cancerous cells.

Menopause

The menopause is a time in your life when the ovaries cease their function and oestrogen levels reduce. The name implies the end of the monthly period 'meno-pause', though symptoms can start before your periods are finally over. The menopause usually occurs between the ages of 45-55, and lasts on average from two to five years.

Not all women experience menopause symptoms and some seem to sail through. Symptoms when they do occur are physical and psychological.

Physically there are hot flushes, night sweats, and the need to empty your bladder frequently due in part to a thinning of the vagina. Psychological symptoms include depression, anxiety, insomnia. Some women experience poor self esteem, low energy levels, lowered libido and panic attacks.

How can you help yourself during the menopause years? Learning about the menopause is important. Exercise is one of very best treatments because it stimulates oestrogen production through the action of your adrenaline glands.

Eating healthily, talking things over with a trusted friend will also help. A growing number of women now take hormone replacement therapy (HRT) for symptom relief. HRT replaces the oestrogen hormone that your body is lacking and so can offset many of the unpleasant side effects of menopause. HRT also guards against osteoporosis and heart disease if taken for at least five years.

While most women are happy with HRT, some women experience nausea or put on weight, or find they don't like taking medication on an ongoing basis. Negative side effects may indicate that the particular formulation doesn't suit. Or a different method – such as a slow-release patch – could be explored. If you do take HRT, your doctor should monitor your blood pressure regularly.

It is now felt that HRT does not contribute to breast cancer, though international medical opinion on this differs. The debate arose due to linkage of the early formulations of the contraceptive pill with breast cancer. Today, the oestrogen dosages in HRT are much lower than used in the pill. While HRT is contraindicated for some women, even those with a family history of breast cancer are being prescribed HRT, with close monitoring. HRT is unlikely to be prescribed without a full medical history being taken, so if going to your GP for HRT, do answer questions accurately.

Many women experience a drop in libido around the time of the menopause, partly due to depression and tiredness. Also, a dry vagina can make lovemaking uncomfortable. HRT will help these physical symptoms, and many women report an increase of desire which arises from an overall resurgence of well-being.

An important benefit of HRT is that it can reduce your risk factors to heart attack and stroke.

Self-help techniques for the menopause include taking Evening Primrose Oil, Royal Jelly or Vitamin B6. Homoeopathic remedies such as belladonna may decrease the flushing, as will cutting down on smoking. While some women swear by complementary therapies, their efficacy is not universally accepted and there are differences of opinion about the value of conventional and complementary approaches in tackling the menopause.

Osteoporosis

The greatest risk factor for osteoporosis is being a woman. The disease is up to six times more common in women than in men because as a woman you develop less bone mass then a man, and because after menopause you lose your ability to retain bone calcium. It's calcium that keeps bones strong, dense and rigid. With less calcium, as you grow older, you are in danger of bone fracture or osteoporosis.

Osteo means bone and porosis refers to the holes that occur in bone when the structure breaks down. There are 15,000 hip fractures in Ireland each year in women over 65.

Calcium can't be absorbed without the help of Vitamin D. Your body manufactures the vitamin only when the sun shines on the skin, but this ability decreases with age. However, you can help yourself. Sunshine, exercise and taking calcium and Vitamin D helps in the prevention of osteoporosis. A Dublin hospital study among older people found that drinking milk fortified with Vitamin D over six months significantly increased vitamin and calcium levels. The foods which build bones include milk, cheese, yogurt, fresh fruit and vegetables, tinned fish and red meat.

Cancer Support for Men and Women

An aspect of a life-threatening illness is the fear and isolation it can engender. When the illness is cancer-related, these fears can be very real and can create almost as much unhappiness as the physical symptoms.

'Support and Services', a practical guide for cancer patients and families lists cancer support groups. These are local groups all over the country composed of cancer sufferers and their families who come together to give each other encouragement and support.

There are also national groups, typically representing people linked with a similar type of cancer – be it brain tumour, Hodgkin's Disease or facial cancer. There is also a national association for parents of children with cancer.

The booklet is available free from the Irish Cancer Society, 5 Northumberland Road, Dublin 4, Telephone 01-6681855 or Freefone 1 800 200 700.

Health Issues for Men and Women

Strokes

A stroke is a form of paralysis or central nervous disturbance caused by brain damage due to interference with blood supply to the brain. Strokes can be age-related, in that an older person's blood vessels may have hardened which can cause a temporary reduction in the amount of blood reaching the brain.

About four thousand people suffer a stroke in Ireland each year. Depending on its severity, a stroke can effect speech and mobility in whole or in part, and varying rates of recovery are possible.

Preventable risk factors for stroke are similar to those for heart disease. You can lower your risk factors by cutting down on fatty foods and alcohol, cut out smoking, consciously cut down on your stress levels and take regular brisk exercise.

A national Volunteer Stroke scheme was set up in 1983. It aims to help people who have speech and mobility problems as a result of a stroke. For more information, contact The Volunteer Stroke Scheme, 249 Crumlin Road, Dublin 12, Telephone 01-4559036.

Incontinence

One in four of all women and one in ten men will suffer from incontinence at some stage of their lives according to the Department of Health. Even temporary or sporadic incontinence can cause embarrassment and discomfort.

Incontinence is the involuntary loss of urine. Stress incontinence – involuntary leaking - can occur when sudden, temporary pressure is placed on your bladder through laughing, coughing or running. Overflow incontinence is when urine escapes without warning, and urge incontinence is a sudden, overpowering need to urinate.

Incontinence is caused by weakening of the pelvic floor and or bladder muscles. Doctors believe that only a small proportion of people suffering from incontinence look for professional help, due to embarrassment or a belief that nothing can be done. This is not the case. Incontinence can be helped today by bladder training and by pelvic floor exercises. Drug treatment can also be very effective in treating the unstable bladder and is often used in conjunction with bladder training to help you regain control as quickly as possible.

Feet

The foot is a complex structure consisting of 26 bones with ligaments, tendons, blood vessels and nerves. Healthy feet are essential for mobility and balance. Your feet which walk thousands of miles over a lifetime at your bidding rarely get the attention they deserve, unless something goes wrong.

Problems include bunions, corns, hammer toes. Don't go in for DIY chiropody, but visit the chiropodist regularly as part of a general health check. Foot problems may also be related to general health. Signs of arthritis, circulatory and neurological diseases, diabetes are often noticed first in the feet.

Dry skin is a common feature of ageing. Apply moisturiser sparingly. Cut nails regularly with proper nail clippers. As you grow older your nails thicken. Submerge the foot in warm water to soften the nails before cutting. Don't get into the habit of slopping round the house in slippers as these will not give your feet the support they need.

Hearing

Most people experience some hearing loss as they get older, caused by changes in the inner mechanism of the ear, and in fact, from the earliest years, you are losing some of the high pitched sounds. But don't assume that hearing loss is serious or irreversible. It may be caused by wax which builds up in the ear. Your GP can soften the wax before removing it by syringe. More serious ear problems may now have a good outcome, and today microsurgery is used to treat and cure many problems in the inner ear.

If you find you do need a hearing aid, get good advice from the Hearing Aid Centre, National Rehabilitation Board, 25 Clyde Road, Dublin 4, Telephone 01-6689618. And persevere. One doctor advises it can take at least six months to get used to a hearing aid.

Loss of hearing can be isolating and help and support can go a long way. You may also receive practical advice, information on lip reading and general support from The Irish Hard of Hearing Association, c/o St Joseph's, Brewery Road, Stillorgan, Co Dublin.

Sight

Seventy per cent of people over the age of forty wear glasses at some time, mostly for close work. The ciliary muscles in your eye which contract in order to allow the lens to focus on near objects become less flexible with time. Have your eyes tested regularly. When choosing glasses, go to a qualified optician and have a full and comprehensive eye test. Cheap glasses use magnifying glass, but your condition may call for curved lens or some other refinement.

Other problems which can occur with age are cataracts and glaucoma. A cataract is a cloud on the central lens which can be removed by operation. Today the lens can be replaced in situ. People well into their eighties are being operated on successfully for cataract removal. With glaucoma, pressure builds up inside the eye and surgery may be necessary to reduce this.

A detached retina is when the back lining of the eye pulls away in whole or in part. This can happen due to sudden shock or trauma to the body. Today laser treatment can weld back the detached section. So have your eyes checked regularly. An experienced practitioner may spot a potential problem before you become aware of it.

Health Promotion

The Health Promotion Unit has a number of helpful leaflets and brochures available on many aspects of staying healthy at every stage of life. For more information contact the Health Promotion Unit, Department of Health and Children, Hawkins House, Hawkins Street, Dublin 2, Telephone 01-6714711.

Good Health

While this chapter has outlined some of the physical problems that can occur as the body grows older, most people at retirement age can look forward to very many years of good health – particularly if you look after yourself and take normal sensible precautions.

Chapter 5

Fit and Well

Retirement shouldn't mean armchair, papers and soap operas all day

*A*ileen worked in the bank all her life but took early retirement at 51 with no regrets: "For years before I had become interested in complementary medicine. I knew I wanted to do something in the holistic health area".

"Learning again was a new challenge. I have always been a great reader, but reading something to retain it in order to be able to reproduce it for an exam is a different matter". She successfully completed her course and in 1991 opened her own business: "There was some altruism in it, I wanted to give back something of what I had got. From my thirties onward I had been interested in health, spirituality, I have got a fantastic amount from this, and met wonderful people. My work energises me and I think that shines out".

Introduction

Being healthy includes emotional well-being - the ability to deal with problems, big and small, that life presents. Here too many older people score. Ideally youthful enthusiasm has been joined by the wisdom of experience, the ability to be reflective, to learn from mistakes and take the long-term view.

Keeping well in retirement involves taking care of emotional and psychological health, which has implications for life-style now and later.

And as we have seen, all change can be traumatic and retirement can signal profound change. Most people enjoy a happy and fulfiling retirement. But a minority of people die within two years of leaving work. Often there seems to be no medical cause. Doctors call it post-retirement syndrome, a general malaise, leading to psychosomatic ailments, depression and sometimes death. And while the numbers who struggle with retirement are small, growing older does bring its own challenges to our psychological health.

In this chapter, we look at the issues affecting emotional health and at some of the ways we can keep ourselves psychologically fit.

Sexual Enjoyment

Simone de Beauvoir wrote of sexual relations in old age: "Not only is the idea shocking but also comic". In a society that claims to have forged the sexual liberation, the idea of older people being sexually active seems to remain taboo. The effect of this as you grow older may be that you become vulnerable to public opinion and end up being affected by the stereotype that society imposes. You may come to be ashamed of your thoughts and needs and begin to suppress your sexual feelings. You may feel your physical prowess or performance may be in decline. Or as a woman you may begin to feel less physically attractive. Or intercourse may become painful due to changes during menopause. All these factors contribute to poor self-image which further reduces desire and performance.

There are many misconceptions surrounding sex in later life. Among them are that sex is purely for procreation, or built on sexual attractiveness and that romantic love is only for young people.

Age does bring some changes in sexual performance. Boredom, fatigue and worry may inhibit sexual libido. Orgasm may be less frequent. More stimulation may be needed to produce an erection. Anxiety may enter the equation. But even if intercourse is affected by health, people still feel the need to be close, sensual and sexual.

There is evidence that ending sexual activity can lead to emotional loneliness, depression, a further decline in self-image and can have a poor effect on the overall relationship between husband and wife. Sexual intercourse is obviously about much more than procreation. It brings the feeling of being needed and wanted. Once the need for contraception has ended, your sexual relationship can be more relaxing and satisfying. For women, menopause far from marking the end to sexual response often brings a substantial upsurge of sexual enjoyment for its own sake.

If your sexual life is not what it used to be and one or both of you is dissatisfied with it, try to talk it over, and if necessary, get some help. Some sexual problems are, in fact, relationship problems, which can sometimes be sorted if people can be open with each other. Sometimes, talking together with a professional third party can provide the proper atmosphere to air difficulties. Accord, the marriage counselling service has branches throughout the country, and local parish offices and community information centres have details.

Accord also employ a number of psychosexual counsellors who can help if the sexual difficulties have an emotional or physical component. Accord, All Hallows College, Gracepark Road, Dublin 9, Telephone 01-8370051.

Stress

Stress has been defined as a mismatch between the demands placed upon you, and your ability to deal with them. From this perspective, stress is subjective. What one person will sail through will cause another to gnaw fingernails down to the quick. However, in the league of objective stresses, life changing events, such as retirement, can be significant.

Stress-related symptoms can include high blood pressure, anxiety, ulcers, depression, tension, exhaustion, insomnia and eczema. There is some evidence that sustained stress may play a part in the development of cancer. It's believed that stress can depress the immune system leaving you prey to infections. When under pressure, your body is in a constant state of fight or flight. When you live in this state of arousal for long enough, you begin to show signs of wear and tear.

How can you cope with stress?

- Talk it over. Someone who can help you explore the problem can be a great help.
- Take some exercise. A 20 minute walk three times a week can help to work off life's petty irritations and increase energy levels which stress can deplete.
- Face it. When we run away, our fears can loom larger. Facing them can cut them down to size.
- Take care of yourself. Alternative health therapies such as massage, yoga, acupuncture can help to deal with stress.
- Learn a relaxation technique Deep breathing and conscious relaxation can centre and calm the body.

Relaxing through deep breathing:

- Inhale deeply then breathe out in small puffs so as to empty your lungs of air.
- Then with mouth closed and shoulders relaxed, breathe in deeply and slowly to the count of eight.
- Hold your breath to the count of four.
- Breathe out slowly through your mouth to the count of eight.
- Repeat this cycle five times.

Learning to breathe deeply can help you become more self aware. It's a good way of calming yourself down.

Depression

Clinical depression is much more than the Monday–morning blues. It is a depressive illness which affects mood, concentration, saps energy and enthusiasm, makes you lose interest in work, friendships, relationships, sex, food, and which disrupts your sleeping patterns. It is very isolating, people caught up in clinical depression have likened it to being in a glass room, looking out at everyone else but unable to reach them or be reached.

There are four main types of depression:

endogenous: endogenous means internal. This is a chemical or biological depression which often occurs without apparent cause and has a genetic basis.

manic: the word comes from 'mania' meaning high. This too has a genetic basis. Bouts of depression lasting weeks or months alternate with periods of elation or mania

personality: people with a poor self-image usually suffer from this type of depression in which they compare themselves unfavourably to others or set standards for themselves which they can never reach

reactive: this can follow major stress such as death, financial difficulties, redundancy. Post-retirement depression, (PRD) can hit people in retirement. This is secondary, not primary depression and can affect someone who is normally cheerful and outgoing. It shows itself in loss of appetite, tiredness, listlessness, a withdrawal from social activity.

PRD may not occur immediately after retirement. There can be a delayed reaction, as it can take some time for the reality to hit home.

Over 80% of severe depressions can be treated quickly with professional counselling rather than medication. In a minority of cases, mood-stabilising drugs will be prescribed and will effectively control the illness in most cases. Any psychotropic or sedatives prescribed should be continuously monitored. If given for secondary depression, they should be accompanied by a dynamic ongoing programme of physical and mental activity.

The organisation Aware - Helping to Defeat Depression - was set up in 1985 to help people suffering from depression - and their families. There are now self-help groups throughout the country. Aware is at 147 Phibsborough Road, Dublin 7, Telephone 01-8308449. Aware has a counselling helpline 01-6791711.

Domestic Violence

It has been estimated that as many as one in five Irishwomen have experienced domestic violence, many on an ongoing basis. Women's Aid say that if the definition of violence were broadened to include mental cruelty and verbal violence, the figures could be doubled.

But family violence is still the unknowable committed on the invisible. It is something that happens in secret behind closed doors. We do know that it crosses all classes, professions and income brackets. There may still be some acceptance of the legitimacy of violence in Irish relationships. According to Women's Aid, if a man assaults a woman, a stranger, on the street he can be arrested, but if it's his wife, our attitudes are much more ambivalent.

Women and children are usually the victims of violence, though it is now becoming recognised that men too can be subjected to physical as well as verbal abuse from their wives.

There are nine refuges in the Republic - two in Dublin, one each in Athlone, Limerick, Galway, Waterford, Wicklow, Cork and Sligo.

Women's Aid set up a telephone helpline three years ago. Calls now run at an average 6,000 a year. Analysis of the calls shows that many seek help around legal issues, such as how to take out a barring or protection order against a violent partner. The line is open 10am-10pm each day. The number is Freephone 1 800 341900.

Women's Aid say that abused women do not leave their husbands/partners lightly. Women, particularly middle-aged women, need a lot of support to leave a long-term marriage in which they have invested heavily. Younger women are more likely to leave earlier if violence begins. Marriage counselling can also help a violent marriage where both parties sincerely want change.

MOVE stands for Men Overcoming Violence. MOVE Ireland helps in the setting up and facilitating of local groups for men looking for new, non-violent ways to cope with aggression and conflict. MOVE Ireland's address is Carmichael House, North Brunswick Street, Dublin 7, Telephone 01-8724357.

Insomnia

Up to 15 per cent of the population say they suffer from insomnia. Menopausal women often sleep poorly, and older people can show a tendency towards fragmented sleep. There are different types of insomnia:

initial: difficulty in getting to sleep.

sleep maintenance: waking frequently.

terminal: waking 1-3am and unable to get back to sleep.

Drugs prescribed for sleeplessness have the potential to become both ineffective and addictive. Studies show that certain sleeping tablets can create an addiction in a matter of weeks or months. Long-term users who try to come off such medication too suddenly can experience severe withdrawal symptoms and feel very unwell. To manage sleep problems healthily you should:

- Avoid napping during the day

- Take regular daily exercise early in the day to help obtain deeper, less fragmented, more restorative sleep

- Set and keep to regular sleep and wake times to strengthen your body's natural rhythm

- Avoid stimulants such as tea or coffee before going to bed

- Take a hot milky drink and try to relax before going to bed

- If unable to sleep, get up and do something relaxing. Worrying about going to sleep makes matters worse

- And remember many older people can and do survive on reduced need for sleep.

Holding Back the Years

How you look at any age affects how you feel. Hundreds of factors determine whether you age gracefully, or not. These include genetic inheritance, diet, life-style, stress, pollution and mental attitude.

Smoking can cause some premature skin ageing, according to dermatologists. This is because smoking narrows the tiny capillaries which carry the blood, leading to skin dryness and wrinkles. Alcohol can cause broken veins, as can sun, salt water, harsh wind and strong heat.

The body's metabolic rate slows down with age, so you may have to eat less, or exercise more than ten years ago to retain the same weight. Posture is very important to how you look. If you carry yourself well, everything you wear will hang better. Drink lots of water. This flushes impurities from the body and gives good clear skin and clear eyes.

For women, the old advice to cleanse, tone and nourish the skin is still valid. Distinguish between skin care and make up. Skin care is the important thing, and the make up is only as good as the base you apply it to. Exposure to sunlight speeds up the skin's ageing process. In the sun, use a sun-screen cream to protect it from harmful ultra-violet radiation. The latest generation of sun preparations contain effective sunblocks, the higher the protection factor, (SPF) the more efficient the block.

Life-Style

Exercise

Most people slow down as they age and become less physically active. Try to counteract this by looking for ways to move your body. Use stairs rather than the lift. Don't use the car for short trips, walk instead. Gardening, DIY and housework are all excellent ways of keeping the body fit and active. There are many ways to build in activity if you put your mind to it. Retirement shouldn't mean armchair, paper and soap operas all day.

Doing a warm up before any exercise programme can be a protection against muscle strain. A short walk, walking on the spot, some stretching exercises are a good idea. After exercise, go through the same short programme to cool down.

Walking

Walking is one of the best exercises we have, and these are the benefits it can offer.

- Walking raises your pulse rate and improves the efficiency of heart, lungs and circulation.
- Walking gives a glowing complexion, more energy and can help you feel relaxed
- Walking briskly helps you lose weight. A fast 20 minutes will burn up 100–150 calories.
- Walking helps in the battle against varicose veins.
- Walking regularly steadies blood sugar levels so that you are less likely to crave sugary foods.
- Walking tones the upper body as well as legs if you swing your arms as you stroll.
- Walking maintains the mineral in bone and decreases the risk of bone disease – important as you age, as your bones become more brittle and the risk of fracture increases.
- Walking regularly helps decrease blood pressure because the arteries in the muscles relax.

The golden rule is to walk for pleasure as well as for health because if you enjoy walking you are more likely to stick to the walking plan. Walking with dog, friend or personal stereo can increase your motivation.

How much to walk? To make a significant difference to weight, shape and fitness, you will need to walk briskly for at least 20 minutes four times a week. The following walking plan is designed for the over fifties:

Week	1	2	3	4	5	6	7	8
Miles	1	2	2	2	2	2	2	2
Minutes	30	37	36	35	33	32	31	30
Times per week	3	3	3	3	4	4	4	4

Assessment

If you follow the plan carefully your stamina will gradually increase, and your pulse rate (a good measurement of fitness level) will start to drop.

While walking, note how breathless you become. You may be breathing heavily, but able to hold a conversation. Don't overdo it. If you feel dizzy, stop. Don't push yourself too far, but equally if you enjoy walking and can get into the habit of walking briskly for an hour a day, you are doing yourself a lot of good.

Equipment

Unlike many sports you don't need special equipment for walking apart from a good pair of shoes. These should be flexible light lace up with thick holes and low heels about a quarter of an inch thick, with a well supported arch with a good grip round the heel. If you don't mind splashing out a little, some sports wear manufacturers have developed a shoe for keen walkers designed to provide comfort and support for feet. These are fitted with a plastic spring system which absorbs the shock of your foot as it strikes the ground then springs back into shape.

Go For Life Programmes provide exercise opportunities and challenges for older people. For more information, contact Go for Life, c/o Age & Opportunity, The Marino Institute of Education, Griffith Avenue, Dublin 9, Telephone 01-8370570.

Jogging

Medical opinion is not so positive about jogging. It is felt that latent arthritis will not be improved with jogging. Don't take it up without a proper medical check up, buy shoes which give proper protection, ideally jog on turf or grass rather than on a surface with no give, (as all the vibrations are transmitted through the skeletal frame), and build up gradually in a supervised programme.

Golf

Lots of people take up golf in retirement. You get three hours walking but you don't notice as you're walking with purpose. It has been described as an expensive way of walking to a pub, but many people feel the membership fee gives good value in the social outlets offered by the golf club.

Swimming

Swimming, like walking is a cardiovascular exercise in that it works on the heart and lungs. Swimming is excellent for building muscle strength, suppleness and stamina. Many older people don't know how to swim, but it's never too late to learn.

The number of swimming pools open to the public increases each year, and some establishments offer special discounts to clubs, to members of active retirement associations or to older people.

Alcohol

The definition of risk-free drinking for men has been raised from 21 units a week to 28 units a week in Britain. Risk free drinking for women remains at 14 units or under per week. (A unit is equivalent to a half pint of beer, a glass of wine or sherry. An Irish measure of spirits is equivalent to one and a half units).

Most people drink sensibly, and there are common sense steps to take to enjoy a drink without creating problems:

- Eat before you drink. Try to have a meal or a snack before or with alcohol.

- Remember salty snacks will make you thirsty and more likely to drink more.

- Pace yourself. Decide how much you plan to drink and stick to it.

- Take small sips rather than big gulps.
- Avoid the round system. It usually means you drink too much.
- If out for an evening, alternate alcohol with a non-alcoholic drink.
- Dilute spirits.
- Never drink and drive.

It's important to be aware of how much you drink. Regular drinkers could have an alcohol-free day or days in the week. The object here is to realise that alcohol is habit-forming and to see how you manage without it.

Because alcohol is used as an escape from problems, there is a temptation to turn to it at times of change and crisis in our lives, including retirement. Could you have a problem with alcohol? Have a look at the following questions:

- Do you regularly drink more than the unsafe level?
- Do you gulp your drinks?
- Do you drink when you are angry/sad/bored?
- Do you get drunk when you hadn't intended to?
- Do you need more alcohol than before to get the same effect?
- Is your work suffering because of your drinking?
- Is your family suffering because of your drinking?
- Are you dishonest with yourself and others about how much you drink?
- Do you regularly over-spend on alcohol?
- Do you sometimes forget what you did when you were drinking?
- Do you drink secretly, alone or in the morning?
- Have you tried unsuccessfully to cut down or cut out?

If you can answer YES to even one of these questions, you may consider examining your attitudes to alcohol. You may have the beginnings of a problem which needs action now. One in ten drinkers become addicted (drink compulsively or binge regularly). Alcohol is habit-forming and the more you drink and the more often you drink, the greater the danger of dependence.

Where can you go for help if you feel you have a problem? First, there's self-help. Some people can face up to problem drinking and consciously cut down. To do this, you may have to set goals, develop friendships outside the pub, and take up hobbies and interests that don't involve alcohol.

Some people will need professional help. This may be available from:

- your G.P
- Alcoholics Anonymous
- local hospital
- addiction counsellors attached to local health board or in private practice
- treatment services, day or residential.

Alcoholics Anonymous has branches country-wide. Its headquarters is at 109 South Circular Road, Dublin 8, Telephone 01-4538998.

The aim of counselling is to give people a clearer insight into their condition, and how they cope with difficulties. A comprehensive programme dealing with long-term problems may include one-to-one counselling, group work, relaxation training, and family therapy in which the members of your family become involved in the process.

Women for Sobriety is for women who want to come to terms with their drinking and whose needs may not be met in a mixed-sex group. Women For Sobriety, St Patrick's Hospital, Dublin 8, Telephone 01-6775423.

Smoking

The evidence against smoking is now incontrovertible.

Smoking kills. Smoking is a risk factor in 90% of lung cancers and 30% of all cancers. Smoking also contributes to hardening of the arteries, heart disease, respiratory problems.

Many middle aged and older people who smoke today began years ago when the risks were not so well understood. You may feel there's no point in giving up now, that the damage has been done. But medical research shows that even after decades of smoking, the benefits of stopping show themselves in the immediate and long-term. 20 minutes after you have had your last cigarette, your pulse rate returns to normal. Three days after giving up smoking, breathing is easier and energy levels increase. Five years later your risk of heart attack has halved.

How can you stop smoking? The following points may help:

- Be motivated – the key to success is wanting to stop. Write down your reasons for stopping and decide on a stop date.

- Get in training. Keeping a smoking diary can help pin-point your patterns. How many cigarettes do you smoke per day. When do you smoke them? Where? With whom? What other occupations do you carry out when you smoke? Analysing your social behaviour may help you formulate stop smoking strategies.

- Cut down. Some people find it difficult to begin cutting down before cutting out.

- Cut out. This will be tough at the start. Learn to cope with the three minute crisis, the craving for nicotine peaks for 3–5 minutes at a time then recedes. Hang on.

- Face feelings. You may feel sick, dizzy, tense, irritated. These symptoms are the toxins leaving your body.

- Know of other stop smoking aids which include: nicotine gum, patch and nasal spray, acupuncture and hypnosis.

- Make healthy choices. Try not to substitute sugary snacks for cigarettes. Instead go for a walk, read a book, have a bath, look at a video, do some physical work, 'phone a friend.

- Keep trying. If you don't succeed, try again. Many people take a few attempts before they stop smoking

- Be vigilant. Ex-smokers say it can take years for the craving for nicotine to go, so remain vigilant, especially when under stress, on holidays or other times when you may feel expansive or vulnerable.

Being Overweight

More than one in two Irish people aged 30–69 is overweight while one in ten is unhealthily fat. While being a little overweight is probably acceptable, being way over your natural weight for your size, sex, physique brings undue pressure to bear on your heart, bones, discs and ankles.

There is no magic formula for weight loss. There are no miracle foods, drinks, cures, or machines which cause excess pounds to be shed and to remain shed. Going on a low calorie diet without exercise is ineffective and counter productive. When you begin to eat normally again, the weight lost will pile back on and you may even gain weight. This is because a diet of under 1,000 calories a day throws your body into famine mode. Your metabolic rate (the rate at which you burn fat and convert it into energy) slows down, and your body begins to hold on to its fat cells. When you begin eating normally again, your body may have increased its natural 'fat set' point, to enable it to preserve fats as a guard against future stringent dieting.

The best way to lose weight is to lose it slowly (2.2 pounds a week) by re-educating your eating habits and by exercising regularly. Before you begin any weight control regime, take advice from a dietitian or your GP. One of the best decisions you can make is not to go on a diet but simply change the way you eat.

- cut down on fats contained in milk, butter, cheese, spreads, pates, cooking oil, mayonnaise.
- eat more carbohydrates – breads, potatoes, pastas, cereals, rice.
- eat more fruits and vegetables – high in vitamins and fibre, low in calories

A calorie is a unit of energy and all calories are not equal. Research suggests you burn off calories contained in carbohydrates more effectively than those in fats.

Taking exercise with less fats will achieve slow, gradual but permanent weight loss. Fitness improves your metabolic rate, the rate we convert food into energy. Food metabolises into energy in the muscle, so the more muscle, the better the conversion. Fat burns in an oxygen flame, when you excite your heart beat and bring it up to training zone, (achieved after 15 minutes brisk exercise), you then begin to burn off fat.

Chapter 6

Safe and Sound

"Six out of ten burglars enter a house through a window"

*S*ix years after retirement, Arthur and Sonia moved to the heart of Co Wicklow. "I always fancied a rural type of existence", he says "but during my working life I had to live in a suburban community to be near work, schools and so on. When I retired, we both felt we could move to the country".

The couple have had to adjust to being alone together in a remote setting: "I think it's a time of your life when you accept one another. When you were younger you wanted to change the whole world including your partner. As you get older, you have more sense and learn more acceptance".

Taking Care of the Home Front

Over 9 in 10 older people live in their own homes and most wish to remain there. Ireland has the highest rate of owner- occupation in the EU. However, we share with Britain and France the highest levels of prewar housing in the EU which has implications for conditions and maintenance.

Guarding Against a Break-in

Making your home a safer place to live may involve both a small investment in security and a safety-conscious attitude. First, pay attention to exterior doors. A lock may be only as good and as strong as the door it is attached to. Forced entry is possible if your doors are made from lightweight wood or glass which can be easily kicked in and/or shattered.

Next, see if your locks need upgrading. Old-fashioned surface mounted locks don't offer as much protection as you may need. Beginning with the hall door, you can buy a five-lever mortice deadlock which is sunk into the interior door rim. This allows the bolt to be locked solid in an extended position so that the door can't be forced open. The lock offers anti-drill security cover, double-sided key operation, hardened steel deadbolt and solid steel locking plate, a lock with one thousand key differentials incapable of being picked and immune to skeleton keys. A variety of these locks is available at locksmiths and hardware shops and may need to be fitted by a qualified person.

One of the newer locks has a built in door chain that automatically engages every time the door is opened from the inside. Door viewers are easy to install and allow you to vet callers before opening the door.

Many people protect the front door but forget about side and back doors which could also be fitted with a mortice deadlock. Key operated security bolts are available for door top and bottoms as well. And remember the patio. Sliding patio doors can be lifted from their tracks if not properly secured. Guard against this by fitting security bolts with a push-to-lock mechanism released only by a key.

Windows

Six out of ten burglars enter a house through a window, so merely closing it is not enough. Ground floor windows are particularly vulnerable. Sheet glass can be broken quite easily without too much noise. (In this context, double glazing provides security as well reduced noise levels and heat retention). Even small windows are vulnerable. Once an adult can fit in a head and an arm, it is possible to enter. There are many types of window locks on the market. Key operated locks are best. One model locks the frame to the window. You could also buy a restricter which allows the window to open only minimally.

Special modern snap locks or window guards are also available for traditional sash and casement windows.

Internal Security

The Garda Crime Prevention office advises you to keep a record of the make, model and serial numbers of electrical items, television, videos, cameras and bicycles. Such goods can be secretly marked for identification in case of theft.

In wanting to deter a burglar, should you lock internal doors? A disadvantage is that locked doors could be smashed. However, a four year Irish security study opted in favour of locking inner doors in the hope of isolating the criminal in a particular part of the house, or at least detaining and delaying him. Don't lock expensive delicate items of furniture, as they could be smashed for their contents.

Burglar Alarms

Installing exterior lights and keeping an exterior side door locked may add to your security. In choosing a burglar alarm, security consultants now believe that stand alone alarms which ring for a time and then stop may be ineffective. The better type are linked to a monitoring point or garda station and use a variety of sensors strategically placed on accessible windows and doors. A combination of contact inertia and glass break sensors guard the house perimeters, while motion detectors protect the interior space.

At the heart of many such systems is a 24 hour seven day a week monitoring control centre to which the home is linked. Other refinements are available. A smoke detector alarm and a personal attack alarm is available with all systems.

Before buying, it is important that you choose a reputable security firm who will give effective advice, carry out the work properly and can offer routine maintenance.

Finding a Reputable Company

The Irish Security Industry Association, (ISIA) set up in 1972 to promote proper standards, now represents over 75% of reputable practitioners. Reputable alarms conform to Irish Standard Specification 199 and carry the Q (quality) mark. The ISIA will supply names of members on request. ISIA, 16 Upper Mount Street, Dublin 2, Telephone 01-6610595.

Also the Garda Crime Prevention Unit has a list of reputable firms and will furnish names to the public. The unit has a small permanent exhibition allowing people to examine different types of locks and bolts and to get free advice on what is most suitable for each home. Garda Crime Protection Unit, Harcourt Square, Dublin 2, Telephone 01-4755555

Many insurance companies give a rebate on house and contents insurance premiums if there is a burglar alarm and/or smoke alarm.

Cultivating a Cautious Attitude

The volume of traffic to your doorstep is on the increase. People drop by to read the meter, carry out consumer surveys, sell religion, raffle tickets and a wide variety of goods and services.

Most of these people are exactly who they represent themselves to be. A minority are not. Some may be offering substandard goods at inflated prices or on dubious credit terms. Others may actually be criminals using a spurious reason to cross your threshold to pocket opportunistic cash or valuables, or to return at a later stage to complete the job at leisure. Unfortunately, today's criminals look like everyone else, in fact the point of a conman is that he looks respectable.

Some older people may be vulnerable because they are physically weaker, lonely or too trusting. How can you protect yourself? You can decide not to open the door unless you're expecting someone. You can buy a door chain, a door viewer or limiter as already discussed.

If asked to buy or donate in the name of an organisation, ask for proof of identity. If in doubt, take the telephone number of the organisation, and check that they have collectors in your area on the day. Check credentials with the door chain on before admitting a stranger to your home. Alternatively, ask them to call back or to make an appointment with you through head office.

Under existing consumer law, you have a cooling off period allowing you to change your mind if you feel you have been pressured into buying something by a doorstep seller and want to change your mind. Probably the best advice is - never buy anything at your door.

Vacant Homes

If you have to leave your home vacant overnight or for a longer period, notify your local garda station. Generally speaking, it's best to camouflage the unoccupied look by cancelling papers if delivered. The local post office will hold on to your post if requested. The local garda station will note the fact that your home is unoccupied and may monitor it in your absence.

Crime Trauma

Having your home burgled is a traumatic experience with long-term effects that insurance companies cannot rectify. Even a small break in can cause huge anguish. You can continue to feel frightened, bereaved and violated for weeks, months, even years after the event. Your trust in society has been eroded. You fear it will happen again. You may think you are being watched, become nervous, anxious, depressed, afraid to go out and frightened at home.

The Victim Support organisation can help in these situations. A national organisation with branches country-wide, Victim Support offers emotional and practical support to 6,000 victims of crime each year. Victim Support, 29 Dame Street, Dublin 2, Telephone 01-6798673. There is also a 24 hour helpline 054-76222.

Fire

There are thousands of home fires in Ireland each year. It is important to be alert to how easily fires can start. A towel airing over a cooker, matches left in the reach of children or grandchildren, portable heaters too near to curtains, clothing or bedding can be danger points.

Protection

You lower your risk of home fires by taking the following steps.

Chimneys

Have chimneys swept twice a year.

Kitchen

- Know that most home fires begin in the kitchen.
- Don't dry clothes over lighted cooker rings.
- Keep electric flexes away from cooker rings and hobs.

Many home fires are as a result of untended chip pans. Don't leave a chip pan unattended, don't fill the pan more than one third/one half full. A chip pan can catch fire if the oil is not changed often enough. If there is a chip pan fire:

DON'T try to seize the pan to carry out of doors.

DON'T pour water on to the fire - it may explode.

DO buy a fire blanket and keep it in the kitchen away from the cooker. A fire blanket made from woven non-toxic and fire resistant fibre glass thrown over the pan will deprive the fire of oxygen. Fire blankets cost about £20.

DISPOSE regularly of flammable rubbish and don't let it accumulate.

Electricity

Overloaded plugs and wires may also cause fires.

Your house may need to be rewired.

- Check for frayed flexes and replace if worn.
- Don't repair blown fuses, replace with a fuse of correct amperage.
- Avoid DIY electrical repairs. Pay a qualified electrician.

Gas

- Switch off the supply at the main valve and contact your gas supplier immediately if you suspect a leak.
- If using bottled gas, check that each room with a gas heater has adequate ventilation.

Portable Heaters

- Keep portable heaters well clear of curtains and furniture and placed where they can't be knocked over.
- Don't move gas or oil heaters when switched on.

Electric Blankets

Follow the manufacturer's instructions. This will tell you if your blanket can be left on all night or should be unplugged before getting into bed. Many blankets conform to an international standard heat sensor which turns the blanket off after 35 degrees. Some blankets have an automatic cut out, which would be important if incontinence is a problem.

Cigarettes

- Don't smoke in bed.

Before Bed Check

- Switch off gas supply at the mains.
- Switch off and unplug electric appliances including the kettle, heaters, television/video.
- Place a sparkguard in front of an open fire.
- Empty ashtrays into a metal bin and make sure cigarettes are extinguished.
- Close gas fires at the valve.
- Close doors to all rooms. This will assist in reducing the risk of fire and smoke spreading should a fire start.

Fire Extinguishers

A fire extinguisher which is more than five years old is probably useless unless you have it regularly rechecked and recompressed. Every member of the household should know how to use it. Modern extinguishers are operated in an upright position. You aim the base at the fire and squeeze the handle. Once an extinguisher has been used, even partially, it needs to be recompressed. You are best served by a dry powder type which should carry the relevant British or Irish Standard Approval mark.

Smoke Alarms

75% of fatalities from fires occur in the home. Most people die from asphyxiation, smoke inhalation and carbon monoxide poisoning. A smoke detector responds to minute traces of smoke by sounding an alarm. and can be wired into the home's electric circuit usually interfacing with the burglar alarm, or it can be battery operated. The alarm emits a sound when the battery needs to be changed. Your smoke alarm is best located in sleeping and living areas away from kitchen and bathrooms. You can buy a special smoke detector for the hard of hearing. Some local branches of Macra na Feirme may install a smoke detector free for elderly people.

Home Safe Home

Other pointers. As you grow older, you may need to give more thought to making your home a safer environment. Keep the hall and stairways clear and well lit. Wear shoes, not slippers about the house. Make sure that rugs and carpets are secure and will not trip you up. Floors should not be excessively polished or slippery. Mats and rugs should be non slip. See also advice on adapting a home for someone who has become ill or frail, Chapter 15.

Neighbourhood Watch

Many neighbourhoods today have come together to form a Neighbourhood Watch scheme. This is normally organised with the help of the local gardai. A local committee is elected, members are vigilant and aware of normal comings and goings, so that anything unusual is more likely to be noted. Older or more vulnerable people may be visited regularly. Houses left vacant because of holidays or other reasons are monitored. Leaflets on how to set up and monitor such a scheme are available at local stations, and gardai may also help in resourcing a public meeting called for the purpose of setting up a local Neighbourhood Watch scheme.

Community Alert

In 1984 Muintir na Tire introduced a Community Alert scheme into rural Ireland. It is now up and running in over 700 communities. Basically the scheme is a rural version of Neighbourhood Watch.

New schemes are established and maintained through the help of local gardai and a local committee. Older, vulnerable people are visited, told about the scheme and how it works. The gardai also advise them on home security.

A national survey in 1995 showed that where Community Alert is working well there has been a decrease in personal attacks by 17%, a decrease in burglaries by 25% and a decrease in all crimes by 21%. For more information, contact your local Muintir na Tire branch.

Living Options: Moving Home in Ireland

When you retire, your home is the focus of your life more than ever and so the choice of where you live becomes vital. For some couples, retirement may be the first time in 30 years when major questions about where to live arise. It's tempting to feel that this fresh chapter also merits a complete change of location. Ultimately whether to move or stay is a personal decision. There can be few rules, but there can be guidelines.

First, why move at all? There may be many good reasons to do so. If your pension provision is poor, you may want to capitalise on your single greatest asset, your home. Second, the house that was a tight fit when brimming with children and their possessions may now be too large, and an unnecessary burden to clean and maintain. The garden, if not too large and labour-intensive now, may become so in a number of years, and you may feel you would have more security in an apartment. Many new complexes are guarded by security gates where access is restricted, giving a feeling of safety to its residents.

However, moving house is usually stressful because of the profound change involved. A couple who have gone into a home as young marrieds, reared a family there, and now contemplate moving in retirement, are saying goodbye to the place where they had the most intense experiences, and where so much of themselves has been invested.

There is also the moving away from the familiar, from friends and neighbours, from shops, church and facilities which they know and where they are known.

So moving isn't something to rush into. In assessing your home, answering the following questions may be helpful:

- It may be fine now at 55 or 65 – how suitable will it be in 10 or 20 years time?

- What kind of repair is it in? If major work is needed, can you afford it?

- Has it become too big? Do you use 4–5 rooms only with the rest lying idle? How much time is spent on housework that could be used more enjoyably?

- Are there stairs? Is the home built on a hill? The ground you cover at 65 may make you breathless at 80

- How accessible are you to shops, buses, doctor, church, bank, post office?

The reason most retired people move home is to gain something smaller, easier to keep, convenient to heat, and accessible to amenities. If this is the case, trading down to a smaller dwelling in the same area which would have the advantage of retaining links with friends, clubs and neighbours may fulfil your needs.

How small? Consider carefully how you would manage in a small apartment. Be prepared for the wrench of parting with furniture that has become part of the texture of your life. Realise you may still want a garage, or workshop, a back garden to call your own, or a bit of extra interior space to use as study, sunroom, music room, whatever – so that you don't have to be together all the time.

Our world becomes more localised when we retire and the amenities on our doorstep become very important. So if considering a new area, find out if your hobbies and interests can transfer with you. Can you join the local golf club, or is there already a long waiting list? Is there a bridge club, a library, a cinema?

Some couples move to be nearer to children and grandchildren. This can work out well. It can also cause difficulties if there are differing expectations about the amount of contact between the generations. Don't move too hastily to be near children or grandchildren. It could be that the current level of interaction suits everyone and any more, or any closer, may be too close for mutual comfort.

Moving house, whether far or near, costs money and a lot of the profit made from changing from a bigger to a smaller establishment could be swallowed up with legal costs, auctioneering fees, advertising, transport charges, decoration and furnishings.

It costs nothing to invite a number of auctioneers to visit your home and assess its worth in today's market. You will probably be gratified at how much it has appreciated in price. But this could turn to deflation when you begin house-hunting and realise how prices generally have soared. Take advice from your estate agent on what, if any, and how much work to do on your own home to make it attractive to a prospective buyer. For example, embarking on extensive decoration could be a waste of money as your taste may not correspond with theirs.

Living Options - Living Abroad

A warmer climate, and a pleasant life-style are what attract most retired people to contemplate upping stakes here and heading off into the blue. But as well as the emotional and relationship aspects discussed above, moving abroad will have particular financial implications. If you move to an EU member state the transfer of state pension and certain other benefit rights such as health care, sickness benefit and family allowances should be relatively straightforward. Outside the EU, there may be more red tape - and it will all take time.

Do your homework carefully. Find out the government departments you will need to deal with in your new country - Departments of Health, Social Welfare, Revenue, and so on. Transferred benefits are governed by the rules and regulations of the new country, not the old. What would your new health entitlements be, for example? How do you claim your benefits? Are they sent to you, or do you have to collect them locally? What is involved in opening a bank account and moving investments?

Your Irish occupational pension will be paid in the currency in which it was originally earned and should be sent to you directly. The main disadvantage is the possible currency exchange loss you risk. Also, there may be differentials between the rate of inflation in Ireland and the rate of inflation in your adopted country, causing you to lose out in real terms. Check out your personal tax position to ensure you don't get caught in a double tax trap. And enquire about probate, death duties and inheritance laws. You will obtain some of this information from the relevant foreign embassy.

Chapter 7

Managing Your Leisure

If you haven't got a hobby ...

*J*ohn lives in a nursing home in west Dublin. "It is an exceptional place, they are good and kind and they can't do enough for you. There was a report on the radio some time back about a nursing home where people were abused. I 'phoned up and said, 'they're not all like that', it was important to maintain a balance.

"I have had many hobbies and interests during my life: photography, collecting guns, collecting Irish silver which was sold by weight. You'd be buying something and he would say 'I couldn't let it go for less than three shillings, (15p), you'd beat him down to half a crown, (12 and a half pence).

"I am reasonably content. I think it's damn silly to be anything else, what's the point? As Horace says 'seize the day'. You've got to live in the present and make the best of it".

Approaching Your Leisure

How you handle holidays is a clue to how you will handle retirement. How long before you get bored? Do you lie in the sand and let the world go by? Or are you going spare by day three? In other words, what sort of person are you? Knowing what you need to keep you fulfiled and motivated will help you assess the ways you wish to fill the hours of retirement.

At a recent retirement course, fourteen people were variously involved in the following range of activities: boating, bridge, chess, cookery, cycling, DIY, films, fishing, flower-arranging, gardening, golf, music, painting, piano, photography, reading, restoring old property, scuba diving, shooting, study, swimming, theatre, voluntary work, walking, writing.

Generally speaking, you continue in retirement what you carry into it, but retirement also gives new opportunities. So if you have no particular hobbies or interests, now is the time to begin giving it some thought. Some hobbies are more social than others, (remember that 80% human contact loss when you leave work), so it's important to choose some interests which bring you in touch with other people. This may be particularly important if you are single, or widowed, or divorced or separated.

The options on how to use your time in retirement include continuing to work, hobbies, learning, travel/holidays and voluntary work.

Continuing to Work

Some people continue to work full-time or part-time in retirement. You could look for job opportunities in shops, offices, hospitals, market research organisations, central statistics office, social clubs, local authorities, tourism organisations. One business consultant suggests not waiting too long before tapping into work contacts if you're selling yourself or your skills. The earlier the better.

If setting up on your own, remember you won't have all the support you used to have in the office, such as fax, business cards, lettered stationery, equipment, computers. Again, capitalise as quickly as possible on your contacts. You may only be able to use the company connections for a short time.

An important asset is any professional knowledge that travels with you be it fitter, writer, solicitor, counsellor... Past experience may allow you set up in business where the main investment is time and skills, rather than capital.

If you start your own business, your tax liability will be affected. You need to keep proper records, and may need professional advice on how to set up a book-keeping system and what expenses may legitimately be offset against tax.

Remember that statistically 80% of new businesses fail within one year of start up and over 5% survive only to year five. Investing your lump sum in a business that collapses could mean that you have lost not only your nest-egg but are also left with debts.

Hobbies

The interaction of hobbies and leisure is a big area. Some hobbies can be enjoyed alone, some need another person or group of people. Some hobbies, such as collecting antiques, can cost a lot, and some, like walking or reading, cost very little. Ideally, different hobbies fulfil different needs.

Active Retirement Association

While many older people continue to enjoy hobbies alone or with family and old friends, a growing number are making new friends and discovering new interests through joining their local active retirement association. The first active retirement association, (ARA) was set up in Dun

Laoire, Co Dublin in 1978 with twelve members. Today there are several ARAs in Dun Laoire, and the original association has over 600 members and organises over 30 activity sessions each week. There are now over 100 ARAs in Ireland with numbers growing all the time. Activities vary and each association plans its own programme depending on the wishes of members.

The following types of activities are widely available:

- art, language, music, singing,
- handicrafts such as crochet, dressmaking, embroidery, knitting, needle-craft, tapestry
- DIY, gardening, wine making, woodwork
- debates, discussions, lectures, local history, quizzes
- bridge, board games, chess, darts
- dance, keep fit, indoor bowls, snooker, swimming, table tennis, yoga
- boule, bowls, croquet, horseshoe pitching, pitch and putt, walking
- holidays, outings, socials.

As you will see, this range of activities fulfils needs in retirement for social interaction, creativity, physical exertion and mental stimulation. These activities are available during the day and evening in convenient locations. Put another way, ARAs offer companionship - a wide range of interesting activities - sport, education - holidays - support - information - a sense of belonging.

The concept is self-help. Members draw first on the skills and talents of other members when looking for instructors, tutors, organisers for the many classes and activities.

ARAs benefit the community by raising the status of retired people and older people in general and many associations work voluntarily in their neighbourhood.

In 1985, as the national movement continued to grow, a Federation of Active Retirement Associations, (FARA) was established to co-ordinate this burgeoning movement. In the years since, FARA has spearheaded a new concept of retirement and ageing in Ireland. FARA operates a free information service for active retired and older people. Information is available in relation to relevant national and local organisations, social, cultural and sporting activities, travel and holidays, rights and entitlements for the over 60s.

How can you join an existing association? Contact FARA for the location on your nearest ARA. If there is none, you may be interested in setting one up. If so, support from FARA is available in two main ways:

- FARA will provide you with a comprehensive handbook which gives detailed guidance on setting up an active retirement association. It covers calling an initial meeting, forming a committee, finding premises, planning an activities programme, funding, communications, duties of officers and much more. The Handbook is part of a resource pack.

- You will receive personal support from the FARA Advisory Panel a group of experienced active retirement organisers selected to assist in the formation of new associations. Federation of Active Retirement Associations, 59 Dame Street, Dublin 2, Telephone 01-6792142.

Innovative Ideas

Over the years, a number of innovative schemes have been established by older people for their enjoyment and development.

The LV Book Club

The idea came in the late 1980s via Aontas, who had commissioned a survey into the educational opportunities available for older people, and discovered a library for older people in Leicestershire, England, run in conjunction with Age Concern.

The LV Book Club began in 1989, in Cork. It is open to people aged 55 and over, (hence the Roman numerals LV), its aim is to share a love of books and help people become familiar with the resources of the library.

There are 20 members and a waiting list. The club meets each month in Cork City Library's reference room. Typically, one or two will come with a prepared reading of a piece of prose or poetry which has meant something to them, so there will be reading, personal comment, then discussion.

Most of the members have loved books from childhood. But reading is a solitary activity. The club makes it sociable and allows them share their love of literature and specific books. Guest speakers, local authors, historians may be invited to the monthly meeting. Members have raised funds to provide soft chairs in the library for older people and magnifiers. The LV

Club join Children's Book Week every year through readings with teenagers and story-telling with younger children. The club has also organised music discussions with young people.

The club offers a model for other libraries interested in fostering contact between older library users, and is willing to offer advice to other interested groups. The LV Book Club, c/o Cork City Library, Grand Parade, Cork, Telephone 021-277110.

The Irish Museum of Modern Art

The art group of St Michael's Active Retirement Association began painting together in the 1980s. In 1991 the Irish Museum of Modern Art (IMMA) was established in Kilmainham. Its Education & Community department wished to make the museum as accessible as possible and made contact with the older people's art group. Before the museum opened, group members were invited to submit one painting each as part of the inaugural exhibition.

The submitted work consisted of landscapes, interiors and flower studies. Additionally, the museum had commissioned a photographer to work for two months with the group, photographing the exhibitors and, through a series of taped conversations, exploring their history and interest in painting. The result was that each exhibit was accompanied by a black and white photograph of the artist, plus some personal text. The exhibition was titled 'Inheritance and Transformation', and the combination of work, photograph and reflection gave it a particular depth.

The exhibition drew local people in to the museum and began a relationship with the older painters, which has continued since. The group set up a regular art workshop in the museum and has now worked with Irish and international artists. The IMMA has devised a national strategy promoting access to the arts for older people. This has led to a new way of working, which has since informed the IMMA's approach to the art group. Subsequent exhibitions have featured self-portrait in oils, acrylics and collage as a way of offering a sense of personal history and identity.

Various community and active retirement groups have been invited to the IMMA to meet the art group members who play host and mediate their own work. One of the aims is that the event acts as a resource, both for other active age groups, and for arts administrators round the country, who want to improve their contacts with older organisations.

IMMA offers tours of the museum and an opportunity to meet with members of the Inchicore Active Retirement Painter's Group. The Education & Community Department, Irish Museum of Modern Art, The Royal Hospital, Kilmainham, Dublin 8, Telephone 01- 6718666.

The Dark Horse Project

This project encourages over 55s to commit themselves to 12 months involvement in something completely new for personal fulfilment or to benefit the community. For more information contact the Dublin Health Cities Project, Carmichael House, North Brunswick Street, Dublin 1, Telephone 01-8722278/8722279.

Bealtaine Arts Festival

Ireland's premier arts festival for and by older people is celebrated in May each year. A national festival involving older people throughout Ireland, its theme is celebrating creativity in older age and it aims to make arts more relevant and accessible to older people. The arts featured within Bealtaine include music, painting, dance and drama, film and storytelling.

Bealtaine is co-ordinated in co-operation with national and local cultural institutions by Age & Opportunity, The Marino Institute of Education, Griffith Avenue, Dublin 9, Telephone 01-8370570.

Travel and Holidays in Ireland

At 66 you qualify for free travel on public transport in the Republic of Ireland and to and from Northern Ireland, with some limitations. Free travel applies on city bus services in Dublin, Cork and Limerick from 10am-4.30pm, and after 6.30pm. There are no time restrictions on provincial buses, on trains or on DART.

Many hotels, guest houses, town and country houses and farm houses participate in Bord Failte's Golden Holiday programme which offers discounts as high as 50% to those aged 55 and over. A brochure listing participating establishments and rates is published each year by Bord Failte. Under 55s qualify if accompanying a qualifying spouse. Prices quoted, which include VAT and service charge, usually relate to cost per person based on two people sharing a double or twin-bedded room. In order to avail of Golden Holiday discounted rate, it is important to ask at the time of booking.

Holidays Abroad

In Europe the over-fifties now make over 100 million trips each year. With more money in their pockets and as a result of the booming travel market over the last 20 years, it's a case of 'have pension will travel'. The typical older person who travels is 65, in good health, financially self sufficient, mobile, eager for knowledge and part of a discerning consumer group which represents 20% of the total European travel market.

Travel companies have got the message. Aer Lingus is one of many airlines who provide cheaper fares for over 60's, so it's well worth enquiring when booking a flight or holiday. Increasingly, tourism authorities too are setting out to woo with particular facilities in hotels and resorts. Concessions fall into two main types, either support systems, (such as travel passes) and/or price reductions. Some concessions are dependent on length of stay, season and location.

Once retired, you can have more choice about when you holiday and how long you stay. Travel is generally cheaper off-peak and there can be good winter sunshine bargains, for example, if you can stay a month or longer. Discounts and concessions are also available for sports, residential courses and special interest breaks, leisure and cultural activities, including entry to museums, galleries, exhibitions, concerts and cinemas. Discover your entitlements. Information on concessions for older people can be obtained from local authorities and tourist   information offices, as well as direct from the operators of transport and travel, leisure and cultural activities.

Have your documentation at the ready. If your youthful appearance belies your years, carry the necessary papers to prove your eligibility. Proof of your age or status is usually covered by a valid passport, identity card or pension book. Railcards issued to older people are essential to obtain concessions on train fares abroad. Holders can claim 30% discount on 21 European rail networks, except in Italy, Spain and Belgium. Railcards are available from Iarnrod Eireann in Dublin, and you will receive further information at mainline stations country-wide. Bring your passport, and a passport-sized photograph when applying for the railcard.

Health insurance form E111 valid for one year will allow you to claim the cost of medical treatment across the EU, where this is not already provided free. Enquire about this form at your local health board office.

If taking the car, breakdown coverage is worth considering and some motoring organisations offer age-related rates.

Home Exchange Holidays

Home exchange is becoming an increasingly popular way of having a holiday, be it in Cannes, Cornwall, Connemara or Clontarf. The newest trend is within-Ireland home exchange, for a week, a month or a weekend. For example, if you live in Dublin and would would like to spend a few days in the west of Ireland, you could exchange homes with someone who would like a break in Dublin. The advantages of a home exchange holiday are free accommodation, self-catering facilities, your home taken care of in your absence, your family pets looked after, and the chance to stay in interesting places off the tourist track.

Intervac is a non-profit making organisation which publishes directories several times a year, each filled with swap offers from 30 countries world-wide. There is also an Irish only directory for exchanges within Ireland. You don't have to live in a sweet thatched cottage or mansion to be included. A browse through the current directories show that most of the Irish families wanting to exchange live in semi-detached homes in suburban estates, or outside rural towns.

The Intervac concept is simple. You pay a registration fee and details of your home are published in the directory which is sent to other members world-wide. Interested parties then contact each other direct. Your subscription entitles you to as many swaps as you like in the year. Your listing allows you give detailed information about your home, the kind of holiday home preferred and country or location of choice. Listing indicates what appliances are available, (dryer, showers, dishwasher, video, microwave and so on), number of bedrooms and living rooms, convenience to shopping and public transport, availability of family car. There is information on amenities like beaches, monuments, walks, entertainment and general local facilities.

The Irish Intervac representatives are Hilary & Frank Kelly, Phillipstown, Ballymakenny Road, Drogheda, Co Louth, Telephone 041-37969.

Chapter 8

Lifelong Learning

Universities are actively recruiting mature students

*A*t the age of four, May was on stage singing and dancing and now in her seventies, she is still at it. As a girl she joined the fit ups, the travelling theatre companies: "They were the days when people didn't have cars and we brought theatre to them all over the country. There was no shortage of jobs. Every day in the paper there would be a list of job vacancies, and if you left one company, you had 6-7 job offers to go to".

Now widowed, May lives in retirement in Co Meath where she has helped to develop drama for enjoyment in her local active age group, as well as producing its annual concert.

"I refuse to feel old. I learned to drive at the age of 73 and passed my test first time. I've never been so busy. Now I'm getting round to all the things I wanted to do when I was younger but never had a chance".

Back to the Classroom

About 200,000 adults engage in some form of education each year. Among these are the many people who go back to school after they retire. Some want to keep the grey cells active. Some want to sit exams they never had a chance to do in their youth, some want the challenge of a degree, to learn a new skill, or meet other people. Don't be put off by bad memories of school in the past. Remember you will bring your maturity, judgement, experience to any classroom setting. You've spent years learning in the school of life, and that will stand to you now.

Courses for adults, with no age restriction, are available in vocational, community and comprehensive schools, universities, regional technical colleges, religious institutions and adult education centres throughout the country. And more informal learning opportunities are available for retired people who are members of active retirement associations, and through other innovative schemes.

Funding

A change in grant eligibility in 1993 has been of benefit to mature students. Until then higher education grants were awarded mainly to current Leaving Certificate holders only. Thus, if your Leaving Certificate was obtained years ago, you were deemed ineligible for financial assistance. The change gives mature students in full-time, (usually day) education the same eligibility for funding as today's school leavers.

Most grants are means tested. Depending on means, you may qualify for full or part-fees, and/or full or part maintenance. Funding bodies include higher education authorities, local authorities, European Social Fund, (ESF), and some also award scholarships each year.

Since autumn 1996 if you receive an offer of a college place on a full-time third level course in a publicly funded institution, you will not have to pay tuition fees. Your only fee may be £150 to cover student services, registration and examination costs.

For information on procedures for going to college as a mature student, contact the relevant admissions office, or the handbook of the *Central Applications Office, (CAO), Eglinton Street, Galway, Telephone 091-63318/63269.*

A guide for mature students seeking entry to full-time third level courses, produced by the Curriculum Development Unit of the Department of Education, may also be helpful.

What's Available

If you are generally interested in learning something new and don't know what's out there, the standard expected, or what you might be capable of, you could contact Aontas, the National Association of Adult Education. Aontas promotes learning throughout life. The organisation's database lists over 3,000 adult courses available throughout the country. Aontas provides the following service to the public:

- Annual learning exhibition at which you can see the range of learning opportunities available
- Library and research facilities
- Support for groups interested in getting a course off the ground
- Individual telephone advice and counselling

  Aontas, 22 Earlsfort Terrace, Dublin 2, Telephone 01- 4754121.

Choices

Probably the biggest growth area in adult education is in the number and variety of day courses now available. Very many vocational schools now offer adult morning classes. Some of these are hobby classes, others are second chance education, allowing you to study for Junior or Leaving Certificate, on a per subject basis if you wish.

In addition many community and comprehensive schools ha
adult education evening programmes – where you study anythi
Arabic to aircraft maintenance, from model making to the mandolii
scuba diving to public speaking. Some establishments have a particu
pro-active approach to older students. For example, Pobalscoil Rosmi
Drumcondra, Dublin, offers 'New Tricks', a computer course for mature
students, as well as a course on ageing and retirement. Ashton
Comprehensive School, Cork has keep fit, yoga, lacemaking, patchwork,
painting and drawing classes for older students.

The following schools offer fee concessions to those over 55: St Tiernan's
Community School, Balally, Dublin 16, Colaiste Chiarain, Celbridge, Co
Kildare, and St Clare's Comprehensive, Manorhamilton, Co Leitrim.

Vocational Educational Committees

Most VECs employ an adult education organiser, (AEO) whose job is to
encourage adult learning in the local community by offering courses and
programmes which adults want and will support. AEOs are always
interested in hearing from older people's organisations who would like to
discuss projects relevant to their members.

There are VEC adult education officers in the following locations: Bray,
Carlow, Cavan, Clare, Cork city, Co Cork, Donegal, Drogheda, Dublin city,
Co Dublin, Dun Laoire, Galway city, Co Galway, Kerry, Kildare, Kilkenny,
Monaghan, Offaly, Roscommon, Sligo county, Sligo town, Tipperary
North, Tipperary South, Tralee, Waterford city, Co Waterford, Westmeath,
Wexford town, Co Wexford, Co Wicklow.

VECs offer a huge range of courses which could be divided into five
main categories:

- enjoyment & recreation: such as bridge, dance, flower-arranging, wine
  making and yoga

- personal development: such as assertiveness, coping skills, counselling

- remedial: such as basic languages, maths, literacy

- DIY/income generating courses: such as crafts, hairdressing, upholstery,
  wood joinery.

- career linked courses such as accounting, business, commercial French,
  computers, journalism, Group Certificate or Leaving Certificate,
  management studies, and start your own business.

In addition, some VECs offer courses which are of particular interest to older people such as – Well Being for the Later Years, Local History, Genealogy and family history. Some VECs extend a particularly warm welcome to older people. For example, Co Roscommon VEC offer start up programmes to launch an active age group in the local community. Co Limerick VEC offer special aerobics and craft classes for active retired people free of charge. VECs in Bray, Co Dublin, Kildare, Leitrim, Meath, Monaghan and Sligo offer concessions to over 55s. Carlow VEC publicise its willingness to provide courses to over 55s on request.

No prior qualifications are needed for most leisure adult education courses. Before signing on, find out what will be covered. Many schools/colleges/communities hold an exhibition or open day before enrolment, describing the range of courses on offer. At that time, you can meet teachers and tutors and discuss course content.

For more information or general advice on what's available, contact your local VEC, or your local adult education officer. Or contact Aontas, who have a list of AEOs in the country.

Pearse College

Pearse College, Crumlin, is an adult and further education college established by the VEC, one of the few devoted solely to adult day learning. Their adult education courses include Environmental Studies, Creative Writing, Irish, German, Art, Literature, Media Studies, Gender Studies, History, Catering, Politics and Economics, PE and Crafts. An enjoyable social programme is a feature of this course with public speaking and debates, theatre, history and cultural outings.

Their general studies course is geared for adults who have been away from education for many years. You have an opportunity to study English, Maths, Irish, History, Geography, French, Music, Science, Art and Computers. A certificate is awarded at the end of the course. One and two year Junior Certificate and Leaving Certificate courses in a full range of subjects are also offered.

Pearse College runs short personal development courses in such issues as coping with stress, growing old and assertiveness. Step by step learning in basic English and basic Maths is also available. Their attitude is welcoming, their watchword is access. For more information, contact Pearse College, Clogher Road, Dublin 12, Telephone 4536661/4541544

University of the Third Age

The University of the Third Age (U3A) was founded in France in 1972. Defining the first and second stages of life as childhood/education and adult/work respectively, the third age is one of post-work activity, a time of expansion and stimulation. So the university is not a building but a group of activities, a project, an attitude of mind.

The idea is that older people form themselves into groups to organise their own learning. These are basically self-help groups who decide the subjects they will cover. Sometimes, people within the group have the necessary knowledge and skills to act as tutors. In other cases, groups negotiate teaching time from local colleges or universities.

There are U3A groups in Dublin, Galway, Longford, Roscommon, and Wicklow. Age Action Ireland has received a grant to promote U3A in Ireland. Age Action Ireland, 114–116 Pearse Street, Dublin 2, Telephone 01-6779892.

Higher Education Colleges

Leisure Learning

These include colleges of technology and universities. The extra-mural departments in many universities offer short courses in subjects such as Arts, Philosophy, Literature, Literary Criticism, Irish Studies, Cultural, Social and Women's Studies and many more. Typically these run during the autumn and spring term, and some colleges offer a third short term up to June. University College, Galway's adult and continuing education programme, for example, covers Celtic art in early Christian Ireland, media skills, introduction to the psychology of counselling, writing, literature and Irish.

The Dublin Institute of Technology (DIT) includes the Colleges of Music, Commerce, Technology, Catering, Marketing & Design. There are regional technical colleges, (RTCs) in Athlone, Carlow, Cork, Galway, Letterkenny, Limerick, Dundalk, Sligo, Tallaght, Tralee, and Waterford.

Most colleges of technology have an adult education programme with evening and some daytime courses. These vary from place to place. Letterkenny RTC, for example, offers computer studies, Russian, addiction studies and counselling under its continuing education programme. Waterford RTC's adult education programme includes sport, theology, nursing, safety, health care, information technology and business studies.

Degree Courses

With regard to degree courses at university, DIT or RTC, anyone over 23 is considered a mature student, and there is no upper age limit. While the proportion of mature students studying for a third level degree is tiny, most institutions now have a pro-active attitude to older students. You are welcomed for the dimension you bring to campus - coupled with a new understanding of the importance of second chance education and lifelong learning. Many third level colleges will facilitate you by offering pre-entry advice and counselling.

The university degree courses most popular with mature students lie in the arts and humanities area, and in psychology, social sciences, languages and business. As a mature student in a third level college, you attend lectures, tutorials, use the library facilities, are assessed, submit essays and sit exams like everyone else. Many colleges have a mature students group or society where supportive networks are formed.

University College, Dublin has introduced a Modular Degree Programme particularly suited to mature students. Leaving Certificate qualification is not essential, and nearly everyone who applies is accepted.

This is a part-time (evening) course. It allows you to study for a BA degree at your own pace. There is a wide range of subjects (modules) to choose from, and you can take one or two modules per academic year. Each module must be studied at foundation level first. A pass in each module earns 30 credits, and when 240 credits are accumulated, you graduate with a Pass or Honours BA degree.

The UCD Modular degree does not qualify for grants as it not considered a full time course. You apply through the CAO, (see above) rather than direct to UCD. You should normally apply in the February preceding the Autumn term.

Some of the degree/diploma courses offered in St Patrick's College, Maynooth, Co Kildare may be of particular interest to adults interested in personal, community and spiritual development.

Crossing the Bridge to College

University College, Dublin offers return to learning courses at a number of different venues in Dublin which are designed as a preparation for people who may be interested in going back to full-time or part-time learning.

The National College of Ireland (formerly NCIR), offers four access courses specifically aimed at adults who have missed higher education opportunities in the past. These are certificate courses in Cultural Studies, Social Studies, Women's Studies, Science and Social Development. They are designed to prepare students for university entry. *NCI, Sandford Road, Ranelagh, Dublin 6, Telephone 01-4972200.*

The Dublin Institute of Adult Education offers a one year diploma 'Return to Learning' evening course with two modules – business studies and cultural studies. It is geared to people who want to return to formal learning after a gap and could be used as a university foundation course, if considering going to third level. *Dublin Institute of Adult Education, 3 Mountjoy Square, Dublin 1, Telephone 01-8787266.*

Pearse College runs a university foundation course designed to prepare you for university in the immediate or more distant future. Through familiarity with a range of subjects in lecture/tutorial settings, you build up study, research and presentation skills. Subjects covered include English, History, Philosophy, Politics, Psychology, the Arts. A certificate is awarded to successful students.

Community Education Groups and Networks

There are dozens of voluntary, community-based education groups round the country providing daytime adult education courses in both formal and informal ways. They may set up classes and courses in local schools, community centres and resource centres. Typical courses on offer cover health, creative writing, computers, crafts, literacy, cookery and the underlying emphasis is on personal development through education. There is now a network of such groups, who meet regularly to share information, support and organise workshops and seminars. Aontas has produced a guide to help groups set up their own learning group, and 'Information Pack for Daytime Voluntary Adult Education Groups', is available from Aontas.

Distance Learning

Distance learning is home learning at your own pace, and may include correspondence courses, modules linked to university departments and the BBC Open University programme.

The National Distance Education Centre

Ireland's distance learning centre was established at Dublin City University in 1982. Its aim is to provide access to third level qualifications to adults all over the country.

Courses available through distance learning include degrees and diplomas in arts, sciences and information technology. There are 11 learning centres in the country. Course texts are provided by notes, lectures and text books. All courses begin with a module covering studying techniques, note taking and how to use course texts to your best advantage.

Programmes are developed in co-operation with Irish universities and third level institutions. There is no formal entry qualification for mature students. *National Distance Education Centre, Dublin City University, Dublin 9, Telephone 01- 7045481.*

Open University

Two million people have studied with The Open University (OU) since its foundation in 1969, with over a thousand Irish adults participating at any given time. An OU office opened in Dublin in 1996. There are eight OU study centres in Ireland located at Cork, Galway, Limerick, Kilkenny, Waterford, Athlone and north and south Dublin. OU students come together at these centres to discuss problems and issues with course tutors.

The OU offers a wide range of distance education courses leading to recognised third level qualifications. No previous qualifications are needed, other than being over 18 and resident in the EU. You start by taking a first year foundation course in one of the following: arts, social sciences, maths and science, or technology. After this you can choose from over 130 subject areas, earning points from each completed course towards a degree.

A full degree takes six credits, and gaining a credit normally involves a year of study of about fifteen hours per week. Course materials include texts, software, multimedia materials and kits.

The Dublin office has advisers who will answer your questions about the many courses on offer, and on grant schemes available to Irish nationals. *Open University, Holbrook House, Holles Street, Dublin 2, Telephone 01- 6785399/Open University 40 University Road, Belfast, 7, telephone 08 0232 245025.*

The International Foundation for Adult Education is a non-profit making body established in the Hague to give expression to the wish of mature people to continue to learn and study throughout life. The Foundation offers a diploma in social studies taken over 12-18 months. Grants are available for people aged over 60. *International Foundation for Adult Education, Donna Veldman, PO Box 93, Egliton Street, Cork, Telephone 022-29358.*

'Lifelong Learning, a guide to educational opportunities for older people in Ireland', provides information on organisations, community education groups, networks, distance education programmes, VEC, secondary and third level programmes and special education programmes for older people in Ireland. The guide is a valuable resource for the many older people interested in becoming involved in education after retirement. 'Lifelong Learning' is produced by *Age & Opportunity, The Marino Institute of Education, Griffith Avenue, Dublin 9, Telephone 01-8370570.* It costs £2.50 including postage and packaging.

Chapter 9

Will you still need me when I'm 64?

"Working with young people ..."

*B*ill is a veteran actor and still working: *"The difference between a 9-5 job and the theatre is that you don't stop abruptly at 65. You grow gradually into retirement.*

"I think other people in other professions should have the chance to retire gradually rather than having to cope with such abrupt and total change.

"Older actors often worry that their memory will desert them, this hasn't happened to me. But the body is showing signs of slowing down. The mind may feel 30 or 40, but your old body tells your mind it cannot cope. There are advantages. You get cooler in old age, you don't fly off the handle, you learn to take the more long-term view".

Why Voluntary Work?

Once you retire, and even before, you may feel you would like to give some time to voluntary work. As an older person you bring to it years of knowledge, skills and perhaps experience in a particular field. What you may get back is continued learning, a sense of satisfaction, an opportunity to meet new people and make new contacts.

Working voluntarily can be as formal as becoming part of an organisation for a designated number of hours a week or as informal as shopping for a housebound neighbour. Before starting to look for voluntary work, particularly at the formal end, it's a good idea to put a shape on what you might do. Answering the following questions may be helpful:

What Kind of Commitment?

- What do you enjoy doing?

  You may have a hobby, interest or expertise you want to share. Do you enjoy working as part of a team, on your own, or one-to-one with someone?

- How much time do you want to give?

  Don't overcommit yourself but allocate an amount of time. You can always expand this if you find you want to do more.

- How can you know if the work will suit you?

  When contacting an agency, ask for a job description of the work involved. Do you need training? Is it available?

- Would you like to work with a particular group?

You may be particularly interested in working with young people, or solely with old people. You may feel you would like to do something with people with disabilities, or marginalised groups. Conversely, there may be areas you know you are not interested in, or settings you wouldn't enjoy.

So where do you look? The best place to begin is locally. Your own neighbourhood will have sport, youth, community and women's organisations. There may be services, playgroups, nursing homes, meals on wheels service, and many more facilities already established. Some may need voluntary help on a regular basis.

Check out notice boards in your local library, in supermarkets, the newsagents' windows, your health centre, local newspaper or local directory. Or you may look further afield.

Matching your Skills to the Volunteer Market

Administration

Many voluntary groups need people to help with the day-to-day running of the organisation. The following skills are helpful in this: computer skills, (word processing, spreadsheet, database), book keeping, filing, dealing with correspondence, telephone, reception.

Selling

Voluntary groups also need people to help with fund-raising. The following skills are helpful: selling, public relations, marketing, organisational experience.

Listening/Counselling

Giving people the gift of your time and attention can be very valuable. There are opportunities to visit people at home and in hospital.

People with counselling skills are in demand to work in a variety of voluntary situations - in self-help groups, bereavement support groups and many more. Some organisations offer training.

Teaching

An increased interest in lifelong learning is creating the need and the opportunity for more teachers. So if you have a particular skill or qualification from aerobics to basket-making through to Japanese, woodwork or zither, your skills may be in demand. Organisations to contact include your local VEC, youth group, women's group, or adult education organiser, (contactable through VEC).

Financial

Many small organisations need help with book-keeping, financial projections, fund raising, accounting, financial planning.

National/Local Contacts

Many of the following national organisations with headquarters in Dublin have a country-wide network of groups and associations contactable at local level.

A-Z of Relevant Organisations

Accord, (formerly Catholic Marriage Advisory Council), All Hallows College, Gracepark Road, Drumcondra, Dublin 9, Telephone 01-8371151 and local centres.

Amnesty International looks for volunteers to write letters to prisoners of conscience all round the world.
Amnesty International, 48 Fleet St, Dublin 2, Telephone 01- 6776361

An Taisce is a conservation organisation with local branches. Volunteer members participate in committee and administrative work as well as keeping a watching brief on local planning developments.
An Taisce, The National Trust for Ireland, Tailor's Hall, Back Lane, Dublin 8, Telephone 01-4541786.

Barnardo's, the child care organisation, need volunteers to work in day nurseries, in the toy library, in their shops, creche.
Barnardo's, Christchurch Square, Dublin 8 Telephone 01-4530355

Community Information Centres provide information and assistance in relation to social services. These are run by volunteers, who receive training. CICs are country-wide. For information about CICs contact the National Social Service Board, Hume House, Dublin 4, Telephone 01-6069000.

Crosscare runs a number of social projects in the Dublin archdiocese. They use volunteers for fund-raising, accounting, and administration.

Crosscare, Catholic Social Service Conference, The Red House, Clonliffe College, Dublin 3, Telephone 01-8360011.

Disability Federation of Ireland, (DFI), is an umbrella body representing over 40 disability organisations country-wide.

DFI, 2 Sandyford Office Park, Dublin 18, Telephone 01-2959344.

Financial Information Services Centres, (FISC) are staffed by qualified accountants who work voluntarily to offer financial advice on taxation, social welfare and debt management to the public.

FISC, 87 Pembroke Road, Dublin 4, Tel 01-6682044

Free Legal Advice Centres, (FLAC) provide some opportunities for volunteers with legal qualifications who give advice to the public.

FLAC, 49 South William Street, Dublin 2, Telephone 01- 6794239.

Friends of the Elderly visit older people, help with repairs to their homes, organise a Christmas party and a weekly club.

Friends of the Elderly, 25 Bolton Street, Dublin 1 Telephone 01- 8731855.

Irish Red Cross Society offers First Aid and Cardiopulmonary Resuscitation courses, as well as training people to care for the sick, in voluntary care and in therapeutic hand care.

Irish Red Cross, 16 Merrion Square, Dublin 2, Telephone 01-6765135.

National Adult Literacy Agency trains people to teach literacy to adults on a one to one basis.

National Adult Literacy Agency, 76 Lower Gardiner Street, Dublin 1, Telephone 01-8553248.

National Social Service Board provides resources to voluntary organisations particularly in the area of information and advice. It also runs training courses, publishes a range of publications and offers a group insurance scheme and pension scheme.

National Social Service Board, Hume House, Dublin 4, Telephone 01–6059000.

National Youth Council, (NYC) runs youth clubs, programmes for young people and raises awareness on issues affecting them. Youth workers receive training.

National Youth Council of Ireland, 50 Pembroke Road, Dublin 4, Telephone 01–6683770.

Refugee Agency organises local support groups for refugees from other countries settled in different areas of the country.

Refugee Agency, 15 Marlborough Court, Dublin 2, Telephone 01– 8787200.

Samaritans offer a 24 hour helpline to distressed or bereaved people. It also have a befriending service. Volunteers are trained and older volunteers are particularly sought. There are branches country-wide.

Samaritans, 112 Marlborough Street, Dublin 1, CallSave 1850 609090 or Telephone 01-8727700

Society of St Vincent de Paul, (SVP) visits people in their own homes and in hospital, offers holidays to children and older people, runs hostels and fund-raising shops. There are local conferences all over the country.

SVP, 8 Cabra Road, Dublin 7, Telephone 01-8384164

Voluntary Service International (VSI) runs workcamps in Ireland and abroad carrying out socially useful work such as constructing playgrounds for deprived young people, or renovating homes and community centres. There is no upper age limit for volunteers.

VSI, 30 Mountjoy Square, Dublin 1, Telephone 01-8551011

Older People – We Need You

In addition to the above organisations, there are four bodies with a special interest in harnessing the skills and experiences of older people. These are APSO, the mentor schemes operated by the IDA and the National Social Service Board, and the Volunteer Service co-ordinated by the Retirement Planning Council of Ireland. Each scheme has its own ethos.

APSO Senior Service Oversees Programme:

The Agency for Personal Service Overseas, (APSO) operates a Senior Service Overseas Programme which aims to capitalise on the management, professional and technical skills of the over 55s.

The criteria are as follows. You should have had experience at senior executive, professional or technical level, be aged 55 – 70, be physically and psychologically fit, be available to travel at two month's notice and be prepared to undertake briefing and orientation beforehand.

The assignments include technical and professional assistance, feasibility studies, advising on policy directions, appraisal and evaluation of projects, local training, small business expertise management, marketing, and product design.

APSO provides return air fare, insurance and accident insurance cover, a daily allowance to cover living expenses and relevant orientation before departure. Your accommodation is provided by the host country and short-term assignments can last from three weeks to six months. Longer assignments last up to two years. "You need to be able to adapt very quickly and make the best of your situation" says one seasoned senior volunteer. "Loneliness is a problem, so you need to be self-sufficient. You need common sense and to be able to take care of yourself".

For more information contact Senior Service Overseas, APSO, 30 Fitzwilliam Square, Dublin 2. Telephone 01-6614411.

Mentor Programme

The word mentor is from the Greek and means 'experienced and trusted adviser'. The Mentor Programme was set up by the IDA (now Forbairt) in 1988 to match the complementary needs of experienced or retired business people who would like to continue to contribute their skills, and the many businesses that could do with such help. The Small Business Section of the IDA realised that some small firms needed help in marketing, planning, financial control and production, but couldn't pay for it. At the same time a pool of helpers was available in the form of retired people with expertise.

Since its inception, hundreds of mentors have given crucial support to thousands of Irish firms with the consequent benefit to the economy in terms of employment, sales, exports and skills enhancement. The programme is market driven and fills a demand in the market-place. Mentors are not paid as such but receive expenses.

Mentors are classified into panels. For ten official days a year the mentors counsel a company on anything from financial restructuring to packaging, from exporting to personnel problems.

For more information contact the Mentor Programme, Forbairt, 35-39 Shelbourne Road, Dublin 4. Telephone 01-6092110.

Social Mentor

The Social Mentor introduced by the National Social Service Board in 1994 has been linking the skills of older people to the needs of voluntary organisations. It uses an apprenticeship approach – the mentor works with a staff member or group over a number of sessions and trains them in the skills they need.

A panel of mentors has been set up with a range of expertise of use to voluntary organisations in the following areas:

* Management
* Human resource development
* Marketing
* Organisational change
* Finance
* Publicity
* Strategic planning
* Project management
* Conflict resolution

Mentors are paid expenses. As a mentor your expertise will be matched with voluntary organisations interested in development.

For more information, contact Co-ordinator, Social Mentor Project, National Social Service Board, Hume House, Dublin 4, Telephone 01-6059000

Volunteer Service

If you feel you would like to do some voluntary work, but still don't know what, or where, or who to approach, the Retirement Planning Council operates a Volunteer Service (VS) which will point you in the right direction.

The service is run by retired people who are themselves volunteers. They will meet you, give you an idea of the opportunities available, help you decide the type of work you want and make the initial introductions for you.

Some examples of the areas in which the Volunteer Service has successfully placed volunteers include, care of older people, of homeless people and of children, community work, consumer groups and church organisations. VS has links with educational bodies, those working with physically and mentally disabled people, hospitals, prisoner aid, combating poverty groups, seamen's clubs, third world development organisations and more.

For more information contact the Volunteer Service, Retirement Planning Council of Ireland, 27/29 Pembroke Street Lower, Dublin 2, Telephone 01-6613139.

Chapter 10

Understanding Your Pension

"Judgments (not always available) in writing"

" Around the time of my retirement I was looking into a men's outfitters shop window with some friends", recalls Jerry. "One of them said 'I'd say we're on our last suits, and if we mind them, they'll see us out!'. Such was the negative attitude about retirement in those days".

That was 15 years ago and Jerry has bought several suits since. He helped set up his local active retirement association and believes that such groups are a great way of adding value to life after work: "People talk about playing golf and digging the garden. But you can't do that all day. Joining an association gives people an opportunity to get dressed up and go out. Everything helps.

"To be candid, I don't feel old. I don't think about it, I just get on with life".

Pensions for All

A pension is a very important piece in the jigsaw of retirement. Almost everyone is entitled to some kind of pension. If you have little or no income of your own, you will qualify for a non-contributory pension from the social welfare system. If you are employed or self-employed, you may qualify for a contributory state pension. Two other kinds of pension provision that can be made are: retirement annuities which are individual pension schemes for self-employed people and occupational pension schemes, the traditional kind of pension scheme sponsored by an employer on behalf of employees.

State Pension Scheme

A state contributory old age pension, which is not means tested, was introduced in Ireland in 1961. Today the state scheme provides a retirement pension at age 65 to people who qualify. At age 66, qualified PRSI contributors are entitled to a contributory old age pension. Contributory pensions are funded out of social insurance contributions by employers and employees, with a state contribution out of tax revenue. The pensions provided are flat rate (not income related) and remain at a basic level. For a single person, the state contributory pension amounts to somewhat less than one third of average industrial earnings. State pensions are generally increased in line with inflation in the budget each year.

Effectively the state provides a base upon which private pension schemes can build in order to give a reasonable standard of living in retirement. Most Irish schemes are now integrated with the state scheme in that they take account of the state pension benefit in calculating contributions to, and benefits, from the occupational scheme.

For information on non-contributory old age pension schemes other Social Welfare allowances and other entitlements for older people, see Chapter 13 - Knowing Your Entitlements.

Occupational Pension

The occupational scheme is a partnership between employer, employee and state. The scheme enables you and your employer to set aside in a tax efficient way a proportion of your earnings throughout your working life in order to help you maintain your standard of living when you retire. The main purpose of occupational pension schemes set up by employers is to provide benefits over and above state provision for you and your family. Most occupational schemes provide benefit payable in cash, or as pension – or both – if you die in the service of your employer before reaching retirement age. Many schemes also provide cover for dependents on your death or after retiring.

You should understand how your scheme works, what your entitlements are, and know how your pension rights are being protected. Many people do not fully understand how their contributions are converted into a pension on retirement. What happens is that the fund of deferred income which has been built up for you over the years is converted into an annuity by the scheme trustees and is paid as an annual pension for life. An annuity is often secured by the payment of a single premium to an insurance company, and comes to you as a series of regular payments. However, larger schemes do not purchase annuities but pay pensions from the ongoing income of the pension fund.

There are two main types of occupational pension scheme – defined benefit schemes and defined contribution schemes.

Defined Benefit Scheme

The defined benefit scheme is the traditional type of pension arrangement. It is calculated by reference to final pensionable pay and pensionable service, the two factors multiplied by a 'pension fraction' to arrive at your entitlement. It defines clearly the pension and other benefits which will be paid to you and your dependents on retirement. For example:

pensionable pay:	12,000 per year
pensionable service:	40 years
pension fraction:	1/60th
pension entitlement:	12,000 x 40/60 = 8,000.

Defined benefit schemes usually take into account the fact that you will also be entitled to a pension under the state's social insurance scheme and the benefits paid will reflect this.

Although fewer in number than defined contribution schemes, defined benefit pension schemes actually cover many more workers – they are the schemes which operate throughout the public sector and in the larger private sector companies.

Defined Contribution Scheme

Under a defined contribution scheme, the benefits depend on the amount of contributions made and the returns these contributions have earned from investment on your behalf by the pension scheme trustees.

Defined contribution schemes often offer members a quotation which has a target pension. This is to give you an idea of what pension you can expect at retirement. It is based on achieving a certain growth rate a year. Growth rates used for projections of benefits must conform with certain standards laid down by the Irish Insurance Federation. By monitoring fund performances on a yearly basis, you can compare the actual with the projected and see if you are on target for the figures.

The important thing about defined contribution schemes is that benefits are not fixed in advance – for two reasons. First, they will depend heavily on future investment income and on annuity rates when you retire. Second, they give you a lot of flexibility and choice to decide how much of the fund will be used for personal pension, how much to provide for dependants and how much will be put aside to cater for post–retirement cost of living increases.

Giving You More Pension Protection

During the 1980s the collapse of some pension funds leaving the workers high and dry alerted the government to the need for more controls. Before the passing of the Pensions Act 1990, if an employer failed to pay contributions, the trustees had little clout. Now the trustee must ensure as far as possible that the employer's contribution is paid. While the trustees have no legal powers to compel this, they have a statutory duty to prepare an annual report for pension fund members and trade unions. So if there are any shortcomings in the fund, it should become apparent before the pension fund can be put in real jeopardy. The Pensions Board also has power to compel employers to pay any unpaid contributions, (see later in this chapter).

The minimum funding standard is one of the main safeguards protecting the entitlements of members of defined benefit schemes (not defined contribution schemes) under the Act. Basically, the minimum funding standard is an actuarial certification which shows that there are sufficient funds in the scheme to meet specific liabilities in the event of the fund having to be wound up.

Since January 1, 1994 ordinary members may be elected to sit on the board of trustees of their company pension scheme along with the employer-nominated trustees. Trustees must account to members on how the scheme is run. Most trustees appoint a pensions consultant, an insurance broker or life assurance company to look after the running of the scheme, but they remain responsible for ensuring that full information about the scheme is available and that members have access to the information they need. They are also responsible for the investment of the fund's assets, though they usually appoint a professional investment manager to do this work for them.

You Rights as a Pension Scheme Member

Under the terms of the Pensions Act 1990, trustees of occupational pension schemes must give information to members about all aspects of the pension scheme, including their personal entitlements. If you are a member of a defined benefit scheme, you can go to your employer now and find out:

- the amount of benefits payable to you at normal pension age, based on your present salary and how such benefits are calculated.
- the date of your entry into the pension scheme, your current salary and your pension fund contributions paid to date
- your death in service benefits, should you die before you retire
- your survivor's benefits, if any
- other options available to you
- information on additional benefits secured from any additional voluntary contributions (AVCs) you make, or transfers from another scheme.

If you are a member of a defined contribution scheme, you can go to your employer now and find out:

- The accumulated value of the retirement fund to date
- The date of your entry into the pension scheme, your current salary and your pension fund contributions paid to date
- The amount of employer's contribution paid to date
- Your death in service benefits, should you die before you retire
- Your survivor's benefits, if any
- Other options available to you
- Information on additional benefits secured from any additional voluntary contributions (AVCs) you make, or transfers from another scheme.

These are some of the additional questions you may have about your scheme:

- What are my rights if I change jobs? (see Portable Pensions below)
- What benefits do my family get if I die before retirement?
- What benefits do I get if I fall ill and am unable to return to work long-term, or never?
- Is my pension index-linked?
- If not, how will it be affected by inflation?
- In a defined contribution scheme, are the likely benefits based on realistic assumptions of growth?
- In a defined contribution scheme, is there an open market option on retirement? In other words, will you shop around among the different companies/plans for the best annuity for your money at that time?

Additional Voluntary Contributions

Is there anything you can do if, having done your sums, you believe your pension plan will fall short of what you may need when you retire? The answer is yes. You can top up your pension by making additional voluntary contributions, (AVCs) as well as your regular pension payments.

AVCs can be applied to contribute towards particular provisions within your pension scheme. For instance, they can help to provide death-in-retirement benefits if your scheme does not provide this. They could be used to secure post-retirement increase on your pension so it becomes inflation proof to some degree. AVCs are also worth considering if you plan to retire early and your retirement pension has to continue over a longer period.

AVCs also make sense on other grounds. You may claim income tax relief for contributions of up to 15 per cent of your total taxable earnings in any one year. Most pension schemes do not require members to contribute very high percentages of earnings – the most common contribution level is 5% of pensionable pay. It, therefore, makes sense, if you can afford it, to use the available tax reliefs to make AVCs. The higher your rate of tax, the greater the benefit to you.

AVCs are flexible. You can pay monthly, quarterly, half-yearly, or yearly. You can vary the amount you pay and pay in larger sums if you find you have some spare cash.

AVCs are worth considering if you have changed jobs and lose out somewhat in your pension provisions. You may be joining a new scheme too late to qualify for the maximum benefits it provides, and so adding to the fund with AVC's can help to alleviate this problem.

A Portable Pension

For many years, changing jobs often meant losing pension rights, which limited the opportunity to plan a career path. So if you were a member of a pension scheme for twenty years but decided to leave to join another firm, in the past you would get back only your own pension contributions minus 25% tax, and would forfeit the pension rights you had built up.

Under the Pensions Act 1990 you can transfer pension rights if you move jobs – but only as they relate to service from the date of the Act January 1, 1991. The rights are not retrospective. So, strictly speaking, people moving to another company today can transfer only the pension rights built up since January 1991, and not the rights accrued in any previous years.

In fact, many firms allow employees to voluntarily transfer all pension rights. If you are contemplating moving jobs, this is something you should find out about. The Department of Social Welfare has appealed to companies to allow full transferability of past rights.

Transferability of past pension rights was not included in the Pensions Act because it was felt that many schemes could not meet the cost of this transferability in full and immediately. The minimum funding standard is designed to ensure that all schemes are in a position to meet their past service liabilities, and it is generally believed that full preservation of past-service rights will find its way into legislation once the funding standard has been met by all schemes in the first few years after the year 2000.

What about Your Dependents?

Many surviving dependents who might benefit under pension schemes (for example on the death of a member) may know nothing about such entitlements. Under the Pensions Act 1990, pension scheme trustees are obliged to give information about death benefits to beneficiaries, but only when these benefits become payable. Until that time, their obligation to provide information to families and dependents is more limited.

Spouses of members of pension schemes are, however, entitled to write to trustees at any time for the following documents:

- The annual accounts of the pension scheme

- The annual trustee report

- A valuation report prepared by scheme actuary for the purposes of the Pensions Act

- The basic information about the scheme, and the legal documentation which constitutes the scheme.

This information should also be made available, if requested, to other dependants who might benefit in the event of the death of a scheme member.

What if you are separated or divorced?

There are an estimated 70,000 separated couples in the country. According to a Combat Poverty Agency report on the financial implications of marital breakdown, the most significant asset for such couples after their family home is their pension. Today both employers and pension trustees who have the discretion to determine who is the lawful spouse are already being called upon to make such judgements when it comes to the disposal of a death in service or retirement benefit.

Where a Deed of Separation is being drawn up by solicitors for a separating couple, (or when engaged in mediation), the question of pension entitlements needs to be addressed. At the time of separation the parties need to be aware of pension scheme entitlements of either or both parties. The benefits made under a private scheme can only be adjusted with a court order, not by a Deed of Separation.

Already a battery of orders under the Judicial Separation Act allow separating couples to settle most aspects of their financial affairs. Where a pension is part of an overall financial settlement, a pension adjustment order can be made by the courts under the Family Law Act 1995. This would involve the court deciding what proportion of the pension or death in service benefit is to be allocated to the spouse or dependent child. Should a pension adjustment order be made, the member's pension on retirement would be reduced by the part designated in favour of the dependant spouse or child. The spouse then has the option of having this paid in instalments as and when the pension falls due, or converted in advance into a single transferable amount. This would then be paid into a separate pension scheme or insurance policy for the dependent spouse.

While opting for a single transferable amount may be initially attractive in that it offers independence and a clean break with the past, such an option may represent bad financial value. It would be wise for a spouse to seek advice before deciding which course of action to take. You may, if you wish, advise your pension scheme trustees that you are living apart from your spouse, and you could write a 'letter of wishes' which nominates beneficiaries, and sets out how you would like to see your lump sum payments paid out. This 'letter of wishes' is related to the death-in-service and retirement benefits, is simply an expression of your preference and cannot be binding on the trustees. If you nominate a new partner as your beneficiary, whether or not the trustees may comply with your wishes will depend on the rules of the scheme and their own discretion. The 'letter of wishes' is not legally enforceable.

What, for instance, is the legal standing of the first spouse if a pension scheme member lawfully remarries? Currently where the Irish courts recognise a foreign divorce or grant a divorce, the original spouse is no longer the lawful spouse and loses any rights under the pension scheme as such. On the other hand, a non-divorced spouse may well qualify for benefits even if he or she is no longer dependent on the scheme member. And even after an Irish or a valid foreign divorce, the ex-spouse can seek to have a pension adjusted in certain circumstances.

In Britain where divorce has been legal for many years there is still no consistency in court rulings on the disposal of assets and pensions. Since the passing of divorce legislation, Ireland is now at the beginning of this debate. Emerging legislation needs to be closely monitored to see how it is working in practice. We need to evaluate how court deliberations are being handed down, and to guard against complacency. At present because family law cases are held in private, it is not possible for the media to monitor them. Few, if any, judgements are given in writing by the circuit judge.

The passing of a law to achieve a desired end, as history often demonstrates, does not necessarily mean that the end will be achieved. There will be a need for vigilance. But this will not be possible until more written judgements are handed down, a research body is set up and the privacy rule is amended in some way.

There is also a need to recognise the value of accrued pension rights in marital breakdown and divorce and to develop formal practice and guidelines which will be as just and equitable as possible to all parties.

The Pensions Board has produced comprehensive guidelines that incorporate the latest legislation covering separation and divorce. 'Guidance Notes which Cover Pension Provisions of the Family Law Act 1995 and the Family Law (Divorce) Act 1996' is a publication primarily geared for practitioners. Its points are synopsised in a booklet entitled 'A Brief Guide to the Pension Provision of the Family Law Acts'. Both publications are available free of charge from The Pensions Board, 2nd Floor, Holbrook House, Holles Street, Dublin 2, Telephone 01-6762622.

Public Service Pensions

Compulsory retirement in most branches of the public service (excluding judges and elected members of the Oireachtas) is at age 65, though public servants may take retirement from age 60. Your pension is worked out as 1/80th of your final pensionable salary, multiplied by your years of service. Your tax free lump sum gratuity is worked out at 3/80ths of final salary for each year of service. In terms of maximum benefits, 40/80ths of your final salary may be payable as pension, with 120/80ths of salary payable as a gratuity.

Pensions increases are reviewed in line with relevant staff salary increases. If you leave to join another state body, you will usually receive full credit for service. If you wish to leave the public service after five years' completed service, you will be entitled to deferred benefits payable at pension age. Under five years, there will be a refund of contributions, or a short service gratuity. As a public servant you may make additional contributions to purchase additional years of service credit.

Should you die in service, your dependants would receive a lump sum consisting of 3/80ths of your salary for each year of completed service, plus 50% of pension based on projected service to normal pension date. After retirement, your pension ceases on your death, but your surviving spouse continues to receive 50% of your pension, and your dependent children continue to benefit.

Personal Pension Schemes

There are approximately 200,000 self-employed people in Ireland and only one person in three has done something about their own pension provision, in addition to contributing to the state pension scheme. Since 1988, self-employed people can qualify for a contributory state pension, and this seems to have heightened interest in all types of pension provision. That's the good news. The bad news, however, is that almost two out of every three self-employed people have made no private pension arrangements.

If you are part of that two out of three, what should you do? First, the earlier you do something, the better. In order to provide the pension level which is normally considered to be desirable, (i.e. two thirds of final salary), it is recommended that pension contributions begin by age 32. If it is desired to provide for dependants as well, pension contributions should begin by age 25. Taking out a pension plan is nothing more than investing in a fund that will provide a pension to replace part of your present income when you retire.

The chief determining factor of the cost of that investment is your age at entry to the pension plan. If a fund has to produce a certain level of income at, say, age 65, then obviously the cost per month is less if you start at 30 rather than at 40 or 50. For example, a pension plan producing an estimated annual income of £10,000 in real terms on retirement will cost approximately £300 per month in contributions at age 30. At age 40 the contribution rises to approximately £500 per month to achieve the same fund because of the element of catching up necessitated by the late start. As a rule of thumb, the cost of a pension almost doubles every ten years, so the need to start early is obvious.

However, another way of looking at pension provision, is that you pay what you can afford, when you can afford it, in the knowledge that such investment is very tax efficient. So while the earlier you start contributing the better, it's also true that it's almost never too late to start. You can contribute up to fifteen percent of your annual income tax free to your personal pension fund, and this provides one of the most tax efficient forms of investment.

Contributions are invested on your behalf in a pension fund whose ultimate value will depend on the level of contributions paid and on long term investment returns. Again the important thing to remember is that the growth in the value of this fund over time is tax free, unlike ordinary savings or investment schemes.

While someone drawing a regular salary every week or month from the employer can predict their income from year to year, the self-employed person may not be able to do this, and so you may need a scheme which takes account of the ups and down of your business life.

There are personal plans which have this flexibility and allow for differing levels of payment to be made at different times. If necessary, payments can be reduced or deferred. If you die before retirement, the value of your fund at death is paid to your dependants.

How to choose a pension company? You could contact an independent broker, accountant, independent financial adviser who specialises in pension planning. A specialist should know of the recent and long term performance of the various pension funds and products, and so will be able to advise you on where to buy your pension plan.

Depending on your age, an adviser may be able to recommend a well balanced allocation of funds into medium/high risk equities in the early years, which give a high yield, and then move to low risk funds as you get closer to retirement. Surveys show that pension funds which constantly move between higher and lower risk investments tend to perform better than personal pensions which rarely move out of 'mixed' managed funds. Small percentage differences in yield can make a big difference in the long run. For example, if you are paying £2,000 pension contribution each year, a 14% yield will give you £44,090 after ten years, and £267,680 after twenty years. The same amount paid into a fund with a yield of 17%, gives £52,400 after ten years and £304,280 after twenty years.

Retirement benefits from a personal pension can be taken at any age between 60 and 70. And you do not necessarily have to stop working in order to take your benefits. At retirement you can use your local accumulated fund to buy a pension. Or you can take up to one quarter of your total fund as a tax free lump sum, using the balance to fund a pension. Part of the available capital can be used to provide a pension for your dependents on your death after retirement.

If you die before you retire, the value of your retirement fund at the date of your death is payable to your dependants. If you become ill in the long-term and cannot work, a permanent health insurance policy can be arranged which will provide an income.

You are also eligible to provide for a personal pension if you work in non-pensionable employment, if you have decided to opt out of your occupational pension scheme, or if you have relevant earnings from another source.

The Pensions Board

The Pensions Board was established in 1990. Its main functions are:

- to monitor and supervise the operation of the Pensions Act and pensions development generally

- to issue guidelines to trustees of schemes on their duties and responsibilities and to establish codes of practice

- to encourage training for trustees

- to advise the Minister for Social Welfare on the operation of the Pensions Act and on pension matters generally.

Pension schemes must register with the Pensions Board which can act on behalf of pension scheme members who are concerned about any aspect of their scheme. The Board can investigate the operation of pension schemes and has the power to prosecute for breaches of the Pensions Act. Individual schemes for self- employed people are not covered by the Act.

The Board deals directly with complaints and enquiries from individual pension scheme members, retired people, employers, trustees, pension consultants and trade unions. Many enquiries are from members querying the amount of information they receive in their scheme. Under the Act, trustees are obliged to disclose to members information about all aspect of the pension scheme and their entitlements. If necessary, the Pensions Board will act on an individual's behalf.

Starting court proceedings is a last resort, but a number of pension schemes have been prosecuted by the Board for failing to meet the deadline for the submission of funding certificates.

The Future Of Pensions

The state pension as we know it may be considerably altered in forty years time. Questions are currently being asked about the future of pensions because of the increasing numbers of people aged over 60 as a proportion of the total population, and the smaller numbers of younger people at work.

It is felt that the future cost of pensions may be too prohibitive to be borne by existing arrangements.

Today's pensions are being funded by the PRSI contributions of today's earners and general taxation. At present there are sufficient working people to support the cost of maintaining pension funds. But according to the Irish Association of Pension Funds, in forty years time the ratio will have fallen. Furthermore, the numbers of people in their mid 80's will increase by over 60%, and some of these will require more expensive and intensive care.

So the cost of funding the state pension will increase. Some analysts predict that funding costs will double by the year 2035. With the costs rising on the one hand, and the number of potential funders falling on the other, things may have to change. One of the most radical suggestions is that future pensions should no longer be provided by the state through compulsory PRSI or by voluntary occupational schemes, but instead should be provided by a compulsory savings scheme in which everyone who works must contribute. The state's role would be to regulate but not operate the scheme. Within this suggestion, unemployed people, or those on low pay would be paid a means-tested pension, funded by direct taxation.

Considerable debate is ongoing on the best method of improving the scope, extent and coverage of pensions, and methods of providing equitable social welfare and occupational pensions are currently under close scrutiny, not least because of the projected shape of our population in the early part of the next century and changing dependency ratios.

Your Rights

Meanwhile, it is worth pointing out again that you are entitled by law to information about your pension, that you should apply initially to your pension trustees for information, but are always free to seek independent professional advice and help if there are pension areas on which you need advice.

Chapter 11

Making the Most of
Your Investment

"Before plunging in, take good advice"

*M*ark will never know if retirement for him meant boredom, carpet slippers and sitting on the sidelines. "The second day after the news of my departure was made public a total stranger contacted me and said: 'you haven't got anything to do now. Please come and help us'."

He has since been voluntarily committed to an urban enterprise scheme which aims to identify and fill gaps in the market and to train unemployed people.

"I get a lot of satisfaction out of it", he said. "You get a great kick out of meeting someone who had been unemployed, hearing their story and realising how they have been helped".

You've Taken the Money, but Where should You Run?

If you decide to take part of your occupational pension as a tax free lump sum, you are following in the footsteps of many retired people before you. However, the range of investment available has increased considerably in the last few years, giving you more choice – and more challenge. In deciding where to invest your money, it is important to examine your circumstances to see which investment best suits your needs. The issues which should inform your decision include:

- the security of capital
- the period of investment
- the ease of withdrawal/potential penalties
- your potential for tax liability/tax savings
- your need for capital growth
- your requirement for income.

Many people investing at retirement age need security, a degree of flexibility, and perhaps periodic injections of further income to combat the effects of inflation on a fixed pension.

Each retired individual or couple will have their own needs. With a good pension, people often decide to invest initially for capital growth. This can change later to an arrangement which gives a regular income. If your pension is low, the lump sum may be needed to provide income right away. If you have retired early, there may be a time gap before you qualify for a state pension, and so may need to top up your occupational pension with income sooner rather than later.

The different institutions in which you could invest your money include the post office, banks, building societies, credit unions, insurance companies, the stock exchange, as well as investing in property, antiques, works of art, or a business venture. What are the differences between each option, and how can you choose?

Post Office

An Post investment schemes are state guaranteed, confidential and tax free and charges free. In addition the post office is local, familiar and convenient.

Post Office Saving Certificates

Saving certificates were first introduced in 1927 to encourage people to save. They have remained very popular, and can be used for either capital growth or income purposes. New issues with new rates of interest are made periodically in response to changing economic conditions and rates of inflation.

Issues may last for many years. The 15th issue introduced in May 1998 provides a guaranteed tax free return of 25% interest over five years and six months. Certificates can be bought in units of £10, up to a maximum holding per person of £60,000. They can be totally or partially cashed in before the end of five years. No interest is paid on certificates cashed within six months of purchase, and interest is added at six monthly intervals only, and not between these dates.

You can, if you wish, take income from these certificates at six monthly intervals. This will produce an income of approximately 5% per year, together with the return of your original investment on maturity.

Issues of savings certificates offer rates of return which are fixed by reference to anticipated long-term of rates of interest at their time of issue. Where there are major changes of climate in the interest rate, a new issue is introduced. Rates of interest for existing issues remain locked in until encashment.

How would a saving certificate work in practice? Taking the May 1998 rate as an example, the returns on an investment of £1,000 after five years and six months are as follows:

	Actual Return	**% Return**
After 1 year	£1,030	3.0%
2 years	£1,063	6.3%
3 years	£1,100	10.0%
4 years	£1,146	14.6%
5 years	£1,210	21.0%
5 years 9 months	£1,250	25.0%

Post Office Saving Bonds

These bonds are often used for capital growth. The bond provides a return linked to the Consumer Price Index, and guaranteed at a minimum rate of return after three years, but may be higher depending on the rate of inflation. The bond can be bought in units of £50 up to a maximum holding of £60,000. You can withdraw the interest after three years at the prevailing rate. The bond can be in joint names, and if you or your spouse dies, the survivor automatically assumes ownership.

Guaranteed minimum returns are changed like those for Saving Certificates in the light of prevailing interest rates, and again existing rates will be locked in until encashed.

Many people use the schemes for long-term investment, and reinvest their money at the end of the designated period. An Post encourages this by offering a slightly increased reinvestment interest rate. However, the maximum reinvestment term is three years. Overall, the advantages of An Post schemes are that they are state guaranteed, tax free and free of charges.

The possible disadvantages are that in a low interest environment, money is locked in at a predetermined rate, which may compare unfavourably to other options which become available.

Before plumping for a particular An Post scheme, it would be important to see what the returns are from the banks and other establishments. Conversely, when considering where to invest, An Post schemes could be used as the benchmark against which other schemes may be compared.

Associated Banks

The main associated banks are AIB, Bank of Ireland, Ulster Bank and the National Irish Bank. Bank investments are secure. Where a scheme with income is required, you can transfer money fairly easily from investment to deposit or current account. You can also avail of other banking services such as cheque book account, laser and credit card, paying bills by direct debit, and having 24-hour access to your cash.

The main commercial banks operate a tiered system of interest rates, depending on the size of investment. Many people place their lump sum in their bank for safekeeping and so that it can earn interest while deciding how to invest it. But generally speaking, bank interest is low, and does not compare well with other schemes. In terms of investment opportunity and return, it is not recommended that your lump sum be placed long-term in a low interest earning account in a bank.

Trustee Savings Bank

The Trustee Savings Bank has a Flexisave Account offering various rates for deposits on demand, also for monies invested for 30, 60 and 90 days. The rate of return depends on the amount and length of investment. Generally speaking, the larger the amount, and the longer the term, the better the interest rate.

Merchant Banks

The merchant banks generally offer fixed rates of interest for deposits normally higher than the associated banks. There is usually a minimum investment amount of £10,000, and again, the greater the investment and the longer the term, the better the rate.

Building Societies

Building Societies offer several types of investment accounts from money on demand, to 60 and 90 day investments. Their rates of interest are normally higher than the Associated Banks. All the building societies offer the facility of monthly or quarterly income.

The main building societies in the country are: The EBS, the Irish Civil Service, (the First National,) the Irish Nationwide. The Irish Permanent

Building Society is now a bank and the First National Building Society will convert to one in Autumn 1998. The building societies offer four different types of accounts: a share account, a deposit account, a monthly income account and a fixed term deposit account. This latter account is not particularly flexible where withdrawals are concerned.

Building societies deduct Deposit Interest Retention Tax, (DIRT) (24% in 1998/99) at source. Because their accounts are not tax-free, the interest rate they offer would need to be extremely attractive in order to compete with other investment opportunities. Again, before investing in a building society account, it would be important to see what other deposit-takers are offering at the time, and compare how your money would fare in another establishment over the same proposed term.

Special Saving Accounts (Tax Incentive Investments)

The Finance Act 1992 allowed for a reduced rate of DIRT of 20% (rather than the standard 24%) on interest on Special Saving Accounts, (SSAs) which comply with certain conditions. This option may be attractive to tax payers, particularly those paying a high tax rate. The tax deducted is treated as satisfying your full liability.

Interest rates vary from one SSA to another and fluctuate on a daily basis. Before investing, it would be important to know that the interest rate is competitive. Care should be taken also in interpreting rates of return. Some companies quote annual rates of return based on non-withdrawals from the fund.

There are conditions. You can invest up to £50,000 only per single account, or £100,000 per joint account. You can hold only one SSA at any one time and with one financial institution – post office, associated bank, savings or merchant bank, building society or credit union. A married couple may have two single accounts or two joint accounts. You can't make a withdrawal within 90 days of opening the account. You must give a minimum notice of 30 days for each withdrawal. The rate of interest is fixed for 24 months only. A special declaration must be completed by the account holder and sent to the Revenue commissioners.

Credit Unions

A Credit Union is a financial co-operative run and owned by its members. Many are run in their local community but some of the largest Credit Unions have an occupation or employer in common.

New legislation governing the operation of Credit Unions came into force in 1997. Under it, a member may now have deposits in the Credit Union in excess of £20,000 and the total amount held by the member shall not exceed £50,000 – or one per cent of the total assets of the Credit Union when aggregated with the amount held in shares.

Loans from Credit Unions are limited to £30,000 or 1.5% of the total assets of the Credit Union, and can now be repayable for periods in excess of 10 years in certain circumstances.

Since Credit Unions are not collectors of DIRT, all income is subject to tax at the individual's marginal rate of tax and should be declared in the normal way on yearly return to the Revenue Commissioners.

Insurance Companies

Guaranteed Income and Growth Bonds are provided by many insurance companies and offer returns that are guaranteed, net of tax and totally confidential.

Guaranteed Income Bonds

Under this contract, a lump sum is invested for a fixed term, usually 3, 4 or 5 years. At the end of the term the original investment is returned. During the term, you can receive a guaranteed tax paid income on a monthly, quarterly, half yearly or yearly basis. However, you cannot withdraw during the fixed term without incurring penalties, and these are highest in the early years of the bond.

In deciding whether or not to invest in a Guaranteed Income Bond, see how they compare to the prevailing bank rate.

Guaranteed Growth Bonds

Guaranteed Growth Bonds are similar to Income Bonds except that the interest is accumulated and paid out to you at the end of the term, together with your original investment. The total return is tax paid as the fund has already paid the tax. It is possible to cash in your bond before the end of the term, but the amount payable may be less. It is important to hold the bond for the term selected. In the event of your death, your original investment together with your accrued interest is paid out to your survivors.

Generally speaking, Income and Growth Bonds are not as attractive as the Post Office Saving Certificate and Saving Bond Schemes. However, occasionally an insurance company will issue such bonds at very competitive rates, and this would be worth investigating, having taken independent professional advice.

Unit Linked Funds

Unit linked funds, offered by most insurance companies, give you access to a wide range of investment opportunities and expertise. A unit linked bond is an open ended investment that you can cash in at any stage. It can be set up to provide you with a regular income, or alternatively you can take partial encashments as required.

There are up to 100 different funds to choose from. They fall into a number of different categories:

Property Fund	invest in shops, offices, factories
Equity Fund	invest in company shares
Fixed Interest ('Gilt')	invest in government securities
Cash fund	invest in cash deposit and short term gilts
International Equity Fund	invest in company shares abroad
Managed Fund	This is the most popular of unit linked funds, and employs a mix of the other sectors

Your lump sum is used to buy units in one or more of a range of investment funds. When choosing particular funds, it is wise to spread the risk. For example, the return on most unit linked bonds is not guaranteed. It could be spectacular, it could be poor, and it depends on the performance of the particular fund selected. Also, the initial charge has to be recouped before the bond begins to make a profit.

For these reasons, you should consider this type of investment only in the long-term, as a 5-7 year investment at minimum. Should you wish to cash in your investment in whole or in part within the first few years, you may lose out because of the set-up, administration and commission charges of up to 5%.

In summary, the main advantages of unit linked bonds are the fact that all returns are tax paid, and that medium to long term they will probably provide a return comfortably in excess of inflation. Also, unit funds may offer an element of capital growth which many investors look for. A disadvantage is the absence of a guaranteed rate of return as unit prices can fall as well as rise. We must also include the financial health warning that entry and exit charges are not always to the investor's advantage.

Unit trusts, operated by banks, work in the same way as the unit funds of the life assurance companies, though there are technical differences between them. Some unit trusts distribute their income to unit holders, others allow it to accumulate. There may also be a liability to tax.

Of all unit linked funds, the 'Managed' or 'mixed' Fund is perhaps the most attractive. It offers an inherent spread of risk with only a small part of your investment being committed to each specialist fund. Overall, unit linked funds could be considered for a small amount of capital. The return is tax paid, as the insurance company has already met income tax and capital gains tax liabilities.

Tracker Bonds

Tracker bonds are lump sum investments offered by banks, building societies and insurance companies. Because of their growing popularity, tracker bonds have become relatively sophisticated, so it would be important to seek advice before investing. The return is linked to the growth rate in the international equity market. Most tracker bonds give a minimum guaranteed return, (typically 10-20% over five years), which is paid even if the stock market index falls below it, so the original investment is protected. In addition, a tracker bond pays a return determined by the growth in an underlying stock market index in world investment markets. These markets include Ireland, UK, Europe, USA, Japan. Tracker bonds are available in issues, meaning that there is a specific closing date before which investments must be in place and they are withdrawn if over-subscribed.

So while the minimum returns are often low, the potential gain could be high – from 75-100% of the growth in the particular equity markets tracked. This return is generally aligned to the performances of any of the following stock exchange indices:

All Ireland Index: tracks the leading companies in the Republic and Ireland

FT 100: tracks the top performing UK companies

S & P 500:   tracks the top 500 shares in the US stock market

Tokyo Stock Price Index: tracks the Tokyo Stock Exchange

European Index: tracks the Stock Markets of Germany, Holland, France and Switzerland.

The investment return is subject to Deposit Interest Retention Tax, (DIRT) at 24%, which is deducted at the end of the term.

The Stock Market

The stock market is a market that buys and sells company shares and gilts. (A gilt is a government guaranteed investment). Whether or not you should consider investing in the stock market depends on the quality of your financial advice, your interest in and expertise in the market, your tax bracket and your ability to offset unused tax allowance against investment.

The most popular investments are the companies which are household names – such as AIB, Bank of Ireland, Waterford/Wedgewood, Fyffe's, Cement Roadstone. These are referred to as blue chip companies. However, the top ten Irish companies account for 75% of the value of the share market, so it can be valuable to mix your investment portfolio to include some smaller companies also – again it's about spreading the risk.

Stock market share prices of publicly quoted companies are listed in *The Irish Times* each Friday, the *Irish Independent* each Thursday and also in *The Sunday Business Post*. Some small investors can derive huge pleasure and interest by following the fortunes of their investment. However, by its nature the stock market is volatile. Prices can fall as well as rise. It can be depressing and worrying at times of falling prices to realise that your investment is shrinking. So if you tend to be a worrier, if you cannot afford to see the value of your investment diminishing, then the stock exchange may not be for you.

There is a school of thought that the stock market and managed funds are never the places for a retirement lump sum because of the element of risk and volatility. **Before plunging in, always take good advice.**

Getting Advice

It is important to be able to receive independent, professional, objective and up-to-the-minute advice on all the many and varied ways you can invest your lump sum. This advice may be available from investment advisers/consultants. Your pension trustee or your personnel office may be able to recommend someone suitable. As a rule of thumb, spread your portfolio. Look at your investments every year, know what's available, and know where to go to find out more.

In the insurance market, you have the choice of dealing direct with an insurance company, an insurance broker (who deals with many insurance companies), or to an insurance agent, representing a specific institution.

A tied agent is allowed to do business only with a single insurance company and you should be aware of this fact if you seek advice from such a person. However, if a tied agent gives you inappropriate advice, the insurance company is responsible for their actions.

What if something goes wrong? The insurance companies in Ireland support and pay for an Ombudsman Scheme under which the Ombudsman will investigate complaints made by individual policy holders. The Ombudsman can recommend appropriate compensation to which the insurance company is bound. Policy holders still not satisfied may have recourse to further action.

Investing in a Business

Investing in a business is not recommended for the unwary or the uninitiated, particularly those relying on their lump sum to augment income.

Surveys show that the majority of small self employed ventures fail within the first year. After five years, only 5% have survived. Be careful not to invest your lump sum in a shaky venture, nor to re-mortgage your house to fund a new business. Bouncing back from a tragedy is far less easy when you're 65 than 35, and your home is a very valuable asset.

Also, be aware if you are appointed a director of a company, even a non-executive or honourary director, under company law you could be liable if someone has been trading fraudulently, or if a venture fails and money is owed.

Many many people are attracted to the idea of investing in a theatrical production – of being 'angels', as such patrons of the arts are called. There are questions to ask before parting with your cash:

- are there any household names in the show?

- will it appeal to the important tourist market?

- how long is the run? Even the most successful production takes some time to break even and recoup production and pre- production costs

- how long are the stars contracted for? The show could slump if they leave early

- what realistic level of seat occupancy is needed to break even?

- what time of the year will the show open?

- what is the track record of the producer/director?

Investing in Property

Ireland's residential property market is driven by the law of supply and demand. Whenever there is a shortage of property coming on the market, and demand remains steady, prices may be inflated. However, artificially high prices tend not to be sustained, and a high is usually followed by a levelling off.

It may be possible to claim the cost of purchasing investment property in certain designated areas as a tax deductible expense. On the other hand, if you have to borrow heavily to buy, your mortgage repayments may be higher than the rental you receive, so it may be some time before you feel the benefit. Also, the market price of some properties can be proportionally higher because of their tax–efficient status.

Investing in property for letting can be troublesome, and many older people may not want to be bothered with the hassle involved. You may attract undesirable tenants, who may damage to your property or refuse to leave. You have the job of collecting the rent unless you pay a property management company to do this for you. The property will have to be maintained, and will incur costs in utilities and other charges.

A Final Say

Finally, it's back to first principles about investments - don't rush into hasty action. Shop around. Take advice from independent professional people, licensed to give that advice.

Chapter 12

Reducing Your Tax Liability

"An inheritance from a Godfather"

V eronica is a musician still hitting the high notes. Her retirement seems to consist of working a nine hour day six days a week. She looks a decade younger than she is, and feels younger still: "I am blessed with energy, I think it comes from loving what I do".

"I absolutely love teaching. I'm enjoying life more than ever these days, and plan to go on teaching till I drop. I get so much back from it, far more than I ever give".

The Tax Net

Income from virtually all sources is taxable. This includes salary as wages, or deferred salary as pension, it includes all long-term social welfare payments, disability benefits, even unemployment benefit is taxable.

Depending on your circumstance, you may be liable for income tax, capital gains tax, capital acquisitions tax, residential property tax, and probate tax.

Tax Exemptions

Certain types of income are exempt from tax. These include the lump sum you choose to take on retirement, and compensation from personal injuries. Also, if your income is below a certain level you may not have to pay tax at all. These levels are called exemption limits, and depend on your age, and whether you are married, single or widowed. As you move into retirement, your exemption limit increases. For example, for 1998/99, if you were under 65, single, and your total income did not exceed £4,100, you were not liable for income tax. Between age 65 and 75, the limit was £5,000. If you were single, aged 75 and over, you would not pay income tax if your total income did not exceed £5,500. The income limits for a married couple are normally double those for a single person in each age classification.

Marginal Relief

Even if your income is above the exemption limit, you may be able to successfully apply for marginal relief from income tax. Marginal relief, (which is tax paid at a special rate), is available to many people living on low incomes. So using the above examples, as a single person aged under 65 with an income tax exemption limit of £4,100, you would be entitled to marginal relief on twice that, ie. £8,200. The maximum tax you would pay is limited to 40% of the portion of your income that exceeds £8,200.

Tax Implications at Retirement

When you retire you may have a change of income level and tax band. There may be new tax free allowances to which you are entitled and you need to know what these are so that you can claim your full share.

You may find yourself moving down to a lower tax band, or dropping out of the tax net altogether due to exemption limits and marginal relief as discussed. When you retire, it is important to notify the tax office, quoting your tax number, so that you can take advantage of any reliefs or benefits which now apply.

Tax Free Allowances

Tax free allowances fall into three categories:

• allowances to which everyone is entitled

• allowances which depend on circumstances and

• allowances which relate to certain expenses.

General Eligibility Tax Free Allowances

The allowances to which every one is entitled include a tax free allowance for being married, widowed or single. The allowance for a single person is half that of a married couple, and widowed person receives somewhat more than half of that of a married couple.

There are age related allowances. If you are aged 65 and over, you qualify for an age-related allowance. All this is doubled if you are married and either you or your spouse is over 65 in the tax year. Also, if you live in privately rented accommodation, you may be able to claim a tax refund on part of your rent.

Special Circumstances Tax Free Allowances

These are allowances which may be available to people suffering from various handicaps or incapacities, or for those caring for such people. If you are a taxpayer maintaining a dependent relative, you may be entitled to a dependent relative tax allowance. You can claim a bereavement tax allowance for five years after the death of a spouse, if you have dependent children. For income tax purposes, a child is considered dependent if aged 16 or under, or over 16 but still in full-time education or in apprenticeship training, or dependent through illness or disability.

Certain Expenses Tax Free Allowances

These are allowances applying to certain expenditures such as medical insurance, rent, employing a person to look after an incapacitated individual and so on.

You get partial tax relief for mortgage interest paid. You may claim tax relief on the interest on repayment of money borrowed for house repairs.

You can also claim tax relief for various kinds of medical expenses, and you may claim tax relief for certain dental and optical expenses.

A 1996 tax allowance on service charges, allows you to claim tax relief on service charges for water and refuse collections.

Income Tax

Income tax is paid at two rates depending on taxable income level. Your gross pay less your tax free allowances equals your taxable income. For the year 1998/1999, a single person with a taxable income up to £10,000, or a married couple with a taxable income of £20,000 would pay income tax at 24%. Taxable income over these two levels was taxed at 46%.

Capital Gains Tax

Capital gains arise from the disposal of your assets. Assets can include property, shares and the goodwill of a business. You are taxed on the gains from such disposals. Disposal refers to the sale, exchange, gift or transfer of assets. It also covers the compensation paid for an asset which has been destroyed or lost.

A gain is considered the net amount of the sale after subtracting the original price and also less certain costs and fees associated with improving the asset, and with the purchase and sale. You are allowed to index your costs to allow for inflation over the period.

The standard rate of CGT is 20%. (There is a 27% rate applying to shares held for over five years in certain unquoted companies). There are exemptions. You do not normally have to pay CGT on the proceeds of the sale of your home, car or livestock.

Also, you do not pay CGT on government stocks, Post Office Saving Certificates or Post Office Saving Bonds, on proceeds of certain life assurance policies or pension funds or on lottery or gambling wins.

The sale of objects worth under £2,000 is exempt from CGT.

There is retirement relief from CGT. If you are over 55 you may be entitled to full relief from CGT if you transfer your farm or family business to your son or daughter. Equally, a transfer to another family member who has worked full-time in the business for five years or more may qualify for relief. The CGT income thresholds are changed each year to allow for inflation.

Capital Acquisitions Tax

Capital Acquisitions Tax, (CAT) comprises two related taxes, gift tax and inheritance tax. A capital acquisition applies to a gift or inheritance. Under certain conditions, if you receive a gift or inheritance, you may be liable to pay tax on it.

The amount of tax is calculated on a sliding scale subject to various conditions as explained below. Depending on these, it is paid at tiered rates from 20% to 40%. Whether or not you are liable to CAT depends on:

A whether gift or inheritance is involved

B the relationship between the giver and the receiver

C the value of the property comprised in the gift or inheritance

D whether any gifts and/or inheritance have been received after June 2, 1982

A - Gift or Inheritance.

Generally speaking it is more tax effective to give someone a gift in your lifetime than have them inherit the same amount after your death. This is because while tax payable on gifts is calculated in the same way as tax on inheritances, tax paid on gifts is 25% lower than that paid on inheritance. However, this discount is forfeit if the donor dies within two years of making the gift.

B - Relationship between giver and receiver

Briefly, the closer the relationship, the less the tax liability. So your spouse is exempt from tax, irrespective of the value of the gift or inheritance. Your children will pay less on the same value of gift or inheritance than would a more distant relation. Where there is no blood relationship, for example, if a non-marital partner is inheriting your estate, liability for inheritance tax would be higher than if s/he were a member of your family.

C The value of the gift or property

The greater the value of your property, the more likely it is that your beneficiary, (excluding your spouse), will incur a tax liability. But again, the value of gift or inheritance that someone may receive from you without being liable for CAT depends on your relationship with the beneficiary. So, for example, your child may pay CAT on only that part of the inheritance over 188,400 at 1998 prices, whereas your niece or nephew may have to pay CAT on a much greater part of the inheritance.

D Prior gifts and inheritances

CAT is calculated on an aggregate of gifts and inheritances rather than taking each as a once off situation. So if, for example, your son received an inheritance from a godfather after 1982, and subsequently receives an inheritance from you, his tax liability on your bequest will take into account the prior inheritance, and will, therefore, be higher.

It would be important to take legal advice when drawing up your will in order to arrange your affairs in such a way as to mitigate your amount of CAT. See also Willing and Able, Chapter 14.

Probate Tax

Probate tax is tax paid by the estate after a death and was imposed in the Finance Act 1993. The rate is two per cent and it applies to an estate with chargeable, (or net) assets of £10,980, (indexed annually). Funeral expenses are deducted from the gross to arrive at net estate value.

There are a number of exemptions to probate tax. Spouses are exempt from probate tax, as is joint property. Property bequeathed to charity is exempt from the tax, gifts, certain insurance policies, pension entitlements and property held in trust are excluded, as is the family home and contents, where the successor is a dependent relative or child.

Insuring Against Tax

Under Section 60 of the Finance Act 1985 it is possible to arrange a qualifying insurance policy for the purpose of paying Inheritance Tax and Probate Tax which may accrue on the death of the insured person. The policy must be in a form approved by the Revenue Commissioners and must be expressly taken out for the purpose of paying the tax. The proceeds of the policy do not form part of the estate and are not themselves taxable. These proceeds must be used to pay tax within one year from the date of the insured person's death

It is possible to decide which tax the policy will pay. It could provide that the policy would pay all taxes, or only Probate Tax, or tax for specific individuals. If arranging such an insurance policy you should seek legal advice. The premium you pay will depend on your age, state of health and size of estate.

Chapter 13

Knowing Your Entitlements

"... you may be entitled to a hearing aid"

*L*eo worked in a busy hospital for 30 years and retirement came as a big shock: "I really loved my work. I looked forward to getting up in the morning. There was always a great buzz, and the feeling that you could help people a little when they were waiting for news, or frightened or worried gave a lot of job satisfaction.

I didn't prepare for retirement. I didn't want to think about it so when it came, it was very hard. I moped around and tried everyone's patience. I didn't know where to put myself. Then I got a health scare and it was the best thing that ever happened. It gave me a fright. It made me realise the good things I still have. Now I say I'm retired and I'm beginning to enjoy it. But it took time. Looking back I should have faced up to it sooner, and prepared before I left work."

Entitlements

Apart from a free travel pass for which everyone over 66 qualifies, there are very few universal benefits for older people. There are, on the other hand, a very large number of payments, grants, types of pensions, benefits and special concessions available from many sources for which you may be eligible. There are conditions attached to each of these which can be quite complex, and can vary considerably from entitlement to entitlement. So don't automatically assume you are, or are not, entitled to some benefit or payment.

Social Welfare and Health Board Payments

These include:

A) social insurance payments which are based on your PRSI contributions, and

B) means tested payments if your income is below a certain level

If you are not entitled to a payment based on your insurance contributions, you may apply for a means-tested payment from the Department of Social Community, and Family Affairs or the Health Board.

Rates of Payment

In the case of social insurance payments, the maximum rates are paid to those who satisfy the qualifying standards in terms of contributions paid and/or credited in the appropriate insurance classes. The minimum rates are paid if you have just enough contributions to qualify.

In the case of means tested payments, the maximum rates are paid if you have little or no means, but it is possible to have some savings and still qualify for some level of payment.

PRSI (Pay Related Social Insurance) Contributions

There are various conditions attached to many of the cash payments. The following are the most important:

Insurance Rates: There are different rates of insurance. Most benefits are available to those insured at the full rate of PRSI, typically if you work in the private sector. Most public servants pay a lower rate of PRSI and are eligible only for Widow's Pension/Orphan's Pension and Deserted Wife's Benefit. Since April 1995, new entrants to the public service pay full PRSI Class A.

Mixed Contributions: If you have paid both a full and modified rate, you may qualify for a mixed insurance pro-rata Retirement or Old Age Pension. Contributions paid in another EU state or a country with which Ireland has a bilateral social security agreement may qualify for benefit or pension under EU rules.

Self-Employment: Most self-employed people began to pay PRSI in 1988. Many are now eligible for the Widow's Contributory Pension and qualify for Old Age Pension from 1998. If you paid contributions, (either employed or voluntary) before 1988, you may qualify earlier.

Self employed people pay PRSI at the class S rate which entitles them to the Contributory Old Age Pension and Widow's Pensions only, subject to their having fulfiled the necessary conditions.

Credited Contributions: If you retire before age 65, you must take steps to keep your contributions up to date. You may do this by:

A Signing on at the Employment Exchange

B Show that you are available, capable and actively seeking work, or retired

C If ill and unfit for work, send in a doctor's certificate to the Department on a weekly basis, or as requested

D If you do not intend to work, if over 55, sign on as a retired person. The necessary form will be sent to your home each year until age 65 or 66 after this initial signing on.

E Become a voluntary contributory. However, this will cost you money.

F. Pay class S insurance if you become self-employed and your income exceeds certain limits.

Note that options A-E will give you a credit equivalent to the class of insurance you were paying when you left work. Class S is a paid contribution only.

Credited contributions are usually given if you are receiving Unemployment or Disability Benefit or Invalidity Pension.

Means Test: Means tests for non contributory payments are complex, and your income from virtually all sources is taken into account. The house you live in is not counted as means unless you get an income from it, by, for example, letting some rooms. In general you cannot give away money or property in order to get a pension, as it may still be counted as means. There is one exception to this – you may give a farm of up to a certain rateable valuation to a child if s/he intends to work the farm.

If you or your spouse is over 66 and you sell your house in order to provide alternative accommodation or to pay nursing home fees, some of the the proceeds from the sale may not, under certain circumstances, be taken into account for the purpose of determining means. However, this exemption will not apply if you move in with family or friends instead of buying a new home or flat.

Dependants: If you qualify for a social welfare or health board weekly payment, you will normally receive extra amounts for adult and child dependants. An adult dependant can be a spouse or non-marital partner. Children up to 18 and living at home are normally regarded as dependants. Young adults up to 22 and in full-time education are normally regarded as dependants. But a child or young adult receiving Unemployment Benefit or Disability Benefit, or social welfare or health board payment in their own right, or with an income of £60 or more a week is not regarded as a dependant.

Pensions And Allowances for Older People

There are three personal pensions payable by the Social Welfare system paid from age 65 to qualified contributors who have retired. These are the Retirement Pension, the Contributory Old Age Pension and the Non-Contributory Old Age Pension. You may receive only one Social Welfare pension at a time.

There are, in addition, a number of allowances for older people.

Retirement Pension

To qualify for a retirement pension you must be aged 65, and fulfil the following conditions:

A Have entered insurable employment before reaching age 55

B Have 156 contributions paid at the above rates if retiring before April 6, 2002

C Have 260 contributions paid if you reach retirement age between April 6, 2002, and April 6, 2012 and 520 contributions paid if you reach retirement age after April 6, 2012.

D Have a yearly average of 48 reckonable contributions recorded since 1953 or first entry into social insurance, which ever is later, for every year up to pension age, to qualify for the full pension. Yearly average of 24 is required for the minimum pension. (A yearly average of 48 from 1979, for every year, up to pension age will also satisfy this condition.)

E Be retired from full-time employment. Any employment undertaken may give only an income of £29.99 per week or less.(Self employment less than £50 per week.)

F Contributions at classes A, E, F, G, H and N count.

Application forms are available from post offices, and completed forms should be sent to *Department of Social, Community, and Family Affairs, Pensions Services Office, College Road, Sligo, Telephone 01-8748444 or 071-69800.*

Early Farm Retirement Scheme

You qualify for this scheme if you are a farmer aged 55-66 who has been actively involved in farming for the past ten years. It allows you draw a retirement income for up to ten years and pass the farm on to your son, daughter, or another beneficiary. You must transfer at least 12.5 acres, but you can retain 2.47 acres for your own use.

In return you get a minimum yearly pension plus a bonus per acre. The income is taxable. The pension expires after ten years or when you reach the age of 70, whichever comes first. The £150m scheme funded mainly by the EU and also by the Department of Agriculture will, in theory, allow up to 7,000 older farmers pass on the family farm while retaining an independent income.

More information is available from the *Department of Agriculture Food & Forestry, Kildare Street, Dublin 2, Telephone 01-6072000.*

Contributory Old Age Pension

To qualify for the Contributory Old Age Pension you must be aged 66 and fulfil the following conditions:

A Have entered reckonable insurable employment before reaching age 56

B Have 156 contributions paid at the above rates if retiring before April 6, 2002, or

C Have 260 contributions paid if you reach retirement age between April 6, 2002 and April 6, 2012.

D Have 520 contributions paid if you retire after April 6, 2012.

E Have a yearly average of 48 reckonable contributions recorded since 1953 or first entry into social insurance, which ever is later, for every year up to pension age, to qualify for the full pension. Yearly average of 20 is required for the minimum pension. (A yearly average of 48 from 1979, for every year, up to pension age will also satisfy this condition.)

F Contributions at classes A, E, F, G, H, N and S do count.

A Pro-Rata Standard Contributory Old Age Pension may be paid to those who have 260 reckonable contributions paid, and who satisfy the other conditions when they have an average (per year) between 10 and 20 contributions. Those whose average is between 10 and 14 will receive 50% of the maximum pension, those whose average is between 15 and 19 will receive 75% of the pension.

There is no retirement condition with the Contributory Old Age Pension.

Self-employed people qualify for a Contributory Old Age pension when they have met the contribution requirements. If you have contributions from previous employment, these will count towards qualifying, along with self-employed contribution.

A full qualified adult payment may be paid with both the Contributory Old Age Pension and the Pro-Rata Standard Contributory Old Age pension. A spouse or partner is not regarded as dependent if they have earnings or income more than £60 per week from employment, self-employment, pension, investments, or if they have a payment from Social Welfare or a Health Board, or receive a Fas payment.

Pro-Rata Pension(Mixed PRSI)

People who do not qualify for a standard pension because they have mixed social insurance contributions, full and modified, i.e. Class A or S plus Class B, C or D. may qualify for a small pro-rata pension if they satisfy all the conditions necessary. To qualify you must have:

A started paying PRSI (full or modified) before reaching age 55 (for Retirement Pension) or age 56 (for Old Age Contributory Pension)

B at least 156 weeks PRSI paid at a rate reckonable for Retirement or Old Age Contributory Pension, that is Classes A,E,F, G, H, N and S (From April 6, 2002, those reaching pension age require 260 full rate contributions paid).

C 260 weeks PRSI (full rate) paid or credited since 1953 or 208 weeks PRSI (full rate paid since 1953)

D paid PRSI at a modified rate, (that is Classes B, C, or D)

E have a yearly average of at least 24 weeks PRSI for Retirement Pension (20 weeks in the case of an Old Age Contributory Pension) if all PRSI (both full and modified rate) is taken into account.

In addition from April 6, 2012, a person who has a mixed insurance record will be required to have an aggregate of 520 full rate and modified rate contributions of which not more than 260 may be paid at the modified rate in order to qualify for a pro-rata mixed insurance Retirement or Old Age Contributory Pension.

Because Social Welfare law is constantly changing, it is important to check out the requirements with the Department of Social, Community and Family Affairs who alone have the authority to decide your precise entitlements.

Application forms are available from post offices, and completed forms should be sent to *Pensions Services Office, College Road, Sligo, Telephone 01-8748444 or 071-69800.*

Non-Contributory Old-Age Pension

To qualify you must be aged 66. There is a means test, but you are allowed have some means and still qualify for maximum or reduced pension. Each spouse may qualify in their own right. In the case of married and cohabiting couples, each person's means is assessed as half of joint means.

You should apply four months before reaching 66. Application forms are available from post offices, and completed forms should be sent to: *Pensions Services Office, College Road, Sligo, Telephone 01-8748444 or 071-69800.*

Allowances for Older People

Aged 80 Allowance

If you receive an Irish social welfare pension, you automatically receive an increase on reaching age 80.

Living Alone Allowance

To qualify you must be aged 66 and over, be receiving a social welfare pension and be living completely alone. Apply separately for this allowance to the section of the Department which pays your pension. You need not be living alone in certain circumstances if over age 75.

Pre-Retirement Allowance

To qualify you must be aged 55 or over, be receiving long-term Unemployment Assistance and regard yourself as retired rather than unemployed. There is a mean test similar to that for Unemployment Assistance. Apply at the employment exchange where you normally sign on.

Widow's Pension (Widow or Widower)

Widowed persons may qualify for a Contributory or Non-Contributory Pension. If you are aged over 66 and qualify for one of the above pensions, you may also be eligible for Benefits in Kind such as free electricity allowance, as set out later in this chapter.

Contributory Widow's Pension (Widows/Widowers):

To qualify, you or your late spouse need enough PRSI contributions, and most employed people do qualify, either fully or partially. Also, if your late spouse received a Retirement or Contributory Old Age Pension, you automatically qualify for a Contributory Widowed Persons Pension if widowed. Apply to the *Pension Services Office, College Road, Sligo, Telephone 01- 8748444 or 071-69800.*

Payments Arising from a Death

There are a number of payments which may be payable to survivors and/or dependents when someone dies.

Death Grant

This is a small grant payable on the death of someone who has paid a certain number of social insurance contributions since 1970. It can also be paid on the death of the spouse or dependent child of the insured person. If the death is due to an accident at work, or from an occupational disease, a special funeral grant may be paid instead and there is no PRSI requirement. Apply to the *Death Grants Section, Government Buildings, Ballinalee Road, Longford, Telephone 043-45211 or 01- 8748444.*

Payment after Death of Recipient

To qualify you must be the adult dependant of someone who was receiving a certain social welfare or health board payment. If you qualify you may continue to receive the payment for six weeks after the death. Equally, an adult dependant's allowance or a carer's allowance can, under certain circumstances, be paid for six weeks after the death.

If your deceased relative had a pension book, you should return it to the Department with death notice or death certificate. If s/he was receiving Unemployment Benefit or Assistance, or health board payment, you should notify the relevant body of the death. To qualify for After Death Payment, apply to the section of the Department which made the payment.

Payment for Unemployed People

If you are unemployed you may be entitled to Unemployment Benefit or Unemployed Assistance.

Unemployment Benefit

To qualify you must be aged under 66, unemployed, capable, available and actively seeking work and have recorded a certain number of PRSI contributions. At age 65 you may be eligible for either Retirement Pension or Unemployment Benefit and may receive whichever suits your circumstances.

Unemployment Assistance

To qualify you must be aged under 66, be unemployed and satisfy a means test. If you are entitled to another payment, such as Retirement Pension, you may prefer to seek the other payment. Apply at your local employment exchange.

Redundancy Payments

To qualify you must be aged under 66 and have been made redundant from your place of employment. Redundancy payment is in the form of a lump sum normally payable by your employer. If there is a problem, contact the *Employment Appeals Tribunal Employment Rights, Davitt House, 65A Adelaide Road, Dublin 2, Telephone 01-6614444.*

Payments For People in Poverty

There are a number of health board payments for people who are trying to manage on a very low income, or have little, or no means. These include a Supplementary Welfare Allowance, and Assistance with Rent or Mortgage.

Supplementary Welfare Allowance

To qualify you need to be trying to manage on a very low income or have insufficient means. The weekly allowance is intended to provide a basic minimum income. You may also qualify for a weekly supplement towards rent, food and heat.

An exceptional needs payment may also be available to meet a particular problem such as rent or mortgage arrears, buying household equipment or meeting funeral expenses. Emergency payments may be made following tragedies or accidents. Apply to the Community Welfare Officer at your local health centre. If unsuccessful, you have the right to appeal the decision to the Programme Manager, Community Care, at Health Board headquarters.

Rent or Mortgage Assistance

To qualify you need to be totally dependent on a social welfare payment, but this is a discretionary scheme under the Supplementary Welfare Allowance, so there is no absolute right to assistance. Apply to the Community Welfare Office at your local health centre.

Payment when Someone is Ill or Needs Care

There are a number of payments available to families or individuals who need or give care, or who cannot work due to illness or disability. These include a Carer's Allowance, Disability Benefit, Disability Allowance,

Invalidity Pension, Blind Pension, Blind Welfare Allowance, Mobility Allowance and various allowances or concessions for disabled drivers.

Disability Benefit

To qualify you must be under 66, be unable to work because of illness, and have paid a certain number of social insurance contributions. Within seven days of becoming ill, you must send in a medical certificate (available from your GP) to the Department. This benefit is payable while you remain ill. After that, depending on your PRSI contributions, you may remain on Disability Benefit, or transfer to Invalidity Pension.

Disability Benefit is partly taxable, but the child benefit portion is exempt from tax. You may, at the discretion of the Department, consider transferring to Invalidity Pension, because although it too is taxable, it is paid at a higher rate, and is a passport to other benefits. Apply to the *Department of Social, Community, and Family Affairs, Aras Mhic Dhiarmada, Store Street, Dublin 1, Telephone 01-6797777.*

Disability Allowance (Formerly D.P.M.A.)

To qualify you must be unable to work for at least a year due to a disability. You must also satisfy a means test. If you do not qualify for Disability Benefit, you should apply for Disability Allowance. Apply to the *Department of Social, Community, and Family Affairs, Aras Mhic Dhiarmada, Store Street, Dublin 1, Telephone 01- 8748444.*

Invalidity Pension

To qualify you must have been receiving Disability Benefit and remain unable to work for at least another year.

If you are over sixty, you may be able to qualify immediately for Invalidity Pension depending on your level of social insurance contributions and the nature of your illness. Invalidity Pension is taxable, and Benefits in Kind may be available. At age 65 you may transfer to Retirement Pension, without losing entitlement to Benefits in Kind, and at age 66 you may transfer to Contributory Old Age Pension, if you qualify. Apply to *The Invalidity Pension Section, Department of Social, Community, and Family Affairs, Ballinalee Road, Longford, Telephone 01-8748444 or 043-45211.*

Carer's Allowance

To qualify you must be living with and giving full time care to a qualifying person. A qualifying pensioner may:

* be aged 66 or over

* be aged under 66 and receiving an Irish disability payment of some type, or similar social security payment from an EU or other recognised qualifying country

* be aged 65 and have transferred from invalidity pension to retirement pension

You must also satisfy a means test broadly similar to that for the Non-Contributory Old Age Pension. Apply for an application form the post office or from the *Carer's Allowance Section, Pensions Services Office, College Road, Sligo, Telephone 01-8748444 or 071-69800.*

Occupational Injuries Benefit Scheme

Almost all employees are insured for Occupational Injuries Benefits. The major benefits are:

Injury Benefit - if you are unable to work due to an accident at work or travelling to/from work, or have contracted a work- related disease

Disablement Benefit - if you are unable to work due to a loss of physical or mental faculty caused by an accident at work.

If you have an accident at work you need to fill in a declaration form which is available from *Injury Benefit Section, Department of Social, Community, and Family Affairs, Townsend Street, Dublin 2, Telephone 01-8748444.*

Blind Pension

To qualify you must be blind, and satisfy a means test. You may also qualify for the Blind Welfare Allowance and Benefits in Kind. Apply through your post office or to the *Pension Services Office, College Road, Sligo, telephone 01-8748444 or 071 69800.*

Blind Welfare Allowance

To qualify you must be blind, regarded as unemployable, and satisfy a means test. This is a health board payment operated in conjunction with the *National Council for the Blind, 45 Whitworth Road, Drumcondra, Dublin 9, Telephone 01-8307033.* Apply to your local health board.

Mobility Allowance

To qualify you must have a severe disability which renders you unable to work, but able to benefit from a change of surroundings. You must satisfy a means test, and there are strict medical criteria for eligibility. Apply to your local health board.

Payment for Disabled Drivers/Passengers

To qualify you must be disabled and need to buy and adapt a car in order to get to work. There are grants available from the health board to help you with such costs.

Also, if you are a severely and permanently disabled person who uses a specially adapted motor vehicle as a driver or passenger, you may be exempt from road tax, and/or vehicle registration tax, entitled to a refund on VAT paid when buying your car, and entitled to some refund of the duty you pay on petrol/diesel. Apply to the *Disabled Driver's Section, Central Repayments Office, Office of the Revenue Commissioners, Coolshannagh, Co Monaghan, Telephone 047-82800.*

Disabled drivers are also generally exempt from parking fines. For more information contact *The Irish Wheelchair Association, 28 Blackheath Drive, Clontarf, Dublin 3. Telephone 01-8338241.*

The Disabled Drivers' Association of Ireland provides aids and adaptations for cars and operates a driving assessment centre and driving school. For more information contact the *Disabled Drivers' Association of Ireland, Ballindine, Co Mayo. Telephone 094-64266/64054. Or contact the association at Carmichael House, North Brunswick Street, Dublin 7. Telephone 01-8721671.*

Apply

The best advice, if you think you may qualify for a benefit or payment, is to apply. In general, nobody is going to come along and offer you services. Husbands and wives should each apply for benefits, as should adult family members sharing a household. In many cases, you may be individually entitled.

Appeal

If you are refused a social welfare benefit or receive a lesser amount than expected, you may appeal within 21 days to the *Social Welfare Appeals Office, D'Olier House, D'Olier Street, Dublin 2, Telephone 01-6718633*.

If you have a problem with a Supplementary Welfare Allowance, you should appeal to the Appeals Officer at your local Health Board.

If you are dissatisfied with the outcome of your appeal, you may take your case to *The Office of the Ombudsman, 52 St Stephen's Green, Dublin 2, Telephone 01-6785222*.

Free Benefits

This is the name given to the package of benefits to which you may be entitled if you receive a Social Welfare or Health Board payment and are aged 66 or over. The benefits in kind include free travel, an electricity, gas and fuel allowance, free colour television licence and more.

Free Travel

Everyone over the age of 66 qualifies for free travel. If you are receiving a Disability Allowance or Invalidity Pension you may also qualify. Free travel is available on road and rail services operated by Bus Atha Cliath, Bus Eireann and Iarnrod Eireann, the Aran Islands ferry service, and on certain private services which have opted into the scheme. If you qualify, your spouse may qualify if travelling with you.

There are restrictions on travelling during peak times on some services. Apply to your post office or to the *Pensions Services Office, College Road, Sligo, Telephone 01-8748444 or 071-69800*.

Free Electricity Allowance

To qualify you need to be aged 66 or over and be receiving an Irish qualifying social welfare, old age pension, invalidity, blind or retirement payment, or a garda widow's pension, or similar payment from EU or other recognised country. You may also qualify if you are aged 65 and have moved from an Invalidity to a Retirement Pension.

You must also be living alone, or with a financially dependent spouse or child, or carer, or invalid, or someone who qualifies in their own right. (Note: financial dependency is defined by the Department of Social, Community and Family Affairs, and the criteria can be changed).

If you are aged 75 or over, special arrangements exist. You may qualify or requalify for this allowance, so it is worth applying at this age.

The allowance gives you relief from the normal fixed charges and gives 300 free units per each two month period between October–March and 200 free units per each two month period between April–September. Up to 600 unused units can be transferred to the next billing period. Unused units can be offset against a Nightsaver account.

If you are not a registered consumer but use slot meter electricity you may qualify for a voucher cashable at post offices under a Group Account Scheme.

Apply to the *Pension Services Office, College Road, Sligo, Telephone 01-8748444 or 071 69800.*

Free Bottled Gas Allowance

If you would otherwise qualify for a Free Electricity Allowance but cannot avail of it because you are not connected to the ESB system, you may qualify for the bottled gas equivalent of the electricity allowance. *Apply to the Pensions Services Office, College Road, Sligo, Telephone 01-8748444 or 071 69800.*

Free Natural Gas Allowance

This is an alternative to the Free Electricity Allowance. You qualify for one or other, but not both. You must be a registered consumer of natural gas on the Bord Gais domestic supply. *Apply to the Pensions Services Office, College Road, Sligo, Telephone 01-8748444 or 071 69800.*

Free TV Licence

If you have been awarded a Free Electricity Allowance or Natural Gas Allowance by the Department of Social, Community and Family Affairs, or would qualify for the allowance, but cannot avail of it because you do not have an electricity or gas supply in your own name, you may obtain a free television licence.

Apply to your nearest post office. To claim, bring your current pension/benefit/allowance book AND a recent ESB/Gas bill showing the free allowance AND your most recent television licence.

Free Telephone Rental

This allowance is available to the same groups as are eligible for the Free Electricity Allowance.

To qualify you must be a registered telephone subscriber, living alone or with incapacitated persons, or a child or children under 18 years or age 22 if in 3rd level education, or adult dependant aged 66 or over if you are permanently incapacitated.

If you are aged 75 or over, you may qualify or requalify for this allowance so it is worth applying at this age.

The scheme covers the cost of telephone rental and 20 free call units per 2 month billing period. If you would otherwise be eligible, but don't have a 'phone, you will have to pay the installation charges. (It may be possible under certain circumstances to get help with installation costs under the Supplementary Welfare Allowance Scheme). Apply for free telephone rental to the *Pensions Services Office, College Road, Sligo, Telephone 01-8748444 or 071-69800.*

Free Fuel Scheme (Formerly the free turf scheme)

To qualify you must be receiving a long-term social welfare or similar payment, be living alone, or with a dependent spouse or children, with a carer, or others who meet the conditions of the scheme. This scheme is means tested. The allowance pays a contribution each week towards the cost of home heating from mid-October to mid-April. You may also receive an extra weekly payment if you live in an area with a ban on smoky fuel. Only one fuel allowance is paid to each household.

Apply to the section in the Department of Social, Community and Family Affairs which pays your benefit, or to the local health centre if receiving a health board payment.

Butter Subsidy Scheme

To qualify you must be receiving a means tested payment. You may be eligible for two vouchers per month for yourself and two vouchers per month for each dependant. The vouchers are given automatically to those who qualify. If not received, apply to the section of the Department of Social, Community and Family Affairs which pays your benefit.

Health Services

As well as the entitlements outlined above given largely by the Department of Social, Community and Family Affairs, there are a wide variety of health services including doctor, hospital, treatment and local community services available. Determining your eligibility to free services is largely dependent on your means and whether or not you qualify for a medical card.

Medical Card Holders

To qualify for a medical card you need to satisfy a means test. Means thresholds are updated each January, and if your income is somewhat above the guideline figure, you should still apply, particularly if you have heavy or ongoing medical expenses, or have children, including over 16s in full-time education. As a medical card holder you are entitled to doctor, drug, hospital and other medical services free of charge.

You may be entitled to have travelling expenses to out-patient services and to day hospitals refunded by the health board. The situation here is not uniform but varies between Health Board areas, and has been subject to cut-backs in recent years. Apply to your local Health Centre or Health Board.

You may be entitled to dental and optical treatment from the Health Board. Dental treatment may be provided by a health board dentist or private dentist. Optical treatment may be provided by a health board optician or private optician. Apply to your local Health Board clinic.

You may be entitled to a hearing aid free of charge supplied by the National Rehabilitation Board, if referred from your Health Board. Apply to your Health Board.

You may be entitled to medical and surgical aids and appliances such as wheelchair, walking frame. Apply to your local Health Board.

If You Don't Qualify for a Medical Card

Even if you don't qualify for a medical card, you are entitled to certain health services free of charge. Others are available with a charge, and some of these depend on your circumstances or means.

Public Hospitals

You are entitled to inpatient and out-patient services in a public hospital regardless of income. This means you are entitled to a bed in a public ward and consultancy services and to out-patient services in a public hospital provided that you opt for public health care. There may be charges for inpatient services in a public ward.

If you opt for a semiprivate or private ward in a health board or public voluntary hospital, you must pay the set charges for maintenance and all the treatment costs.

If you attend the Accident & Emergency Department of a public hospital directly, without doctor referral, you may be liable to a charge for a first visit connected with that accident or emergency.

Private Hospitals

Everyone must pay the full maintenance and treatment costs in a private hospital and short-stay nursing home.

Geriatric Departments in General Hospital

A number of general hospitals have specialised geriatric departments. They are not meant for long-term care but deal with medical and other problems of ageing. Your entitlement to services is the same as for hospitals generally.

Long Stay Nursing Homes

There are different kinds of hospitals and nursing homes which cater for older people on a long term basis. Your entitlement depends on the institution. The following is a brief description of the different categories.

Private Nursing Homes

These vary from profit making ventures, to establishments run by voluntary or religious organisations on a non–profit making basis. If you, or a family member need long-term nursing home care, you may qualify for help with the costs. To qualify for such subvention, you must satisfy a means test, show that you are unable to meet the cost, and have been assessed as needing nursing home care by the health board.

The amount of financial assistance you receive will depend on the degree of nursing home care required, your means and family circumstances. The means test will take account of your income and the income of your spouse/partner, and your family. The maximum grant will be paid to those whose only income is the Non-Contributory Old Age Pension, and whose family is not deemed capable of contributing towards maintenance.

All nursing homes must conform to certain minimum legal standards. The Health Board is responsible for ensuring that these standards are met, so you should contact the Health Board if there is a problem. You may be able to claim income tax relief on nursing home fees. For more information, apply to your local health centre, or Health Board.

Geriatric Hospitals

If you are receiving a social welfare pension you are expected to contribute most of it towards your keep. Otherwise, you are expected to make a means-related contribution.

Geriatric hospitals are run by Health Boards.

Welfare Homes

The qualifying conditions are the same as for geriatric hospitals. Welfare homes are also run by health boards.

Long Term Illnesses - Free Drugs and Medicine

To qualify for the necessary drugs and medicines free of charge, you must be suffering from any of the following long-term illnesses: acute leukaemia, cerebral palsy, cystic fibrosis, diabetes mellitus, epilepsy, haemophilia, mental handicap, multiple sclerosis, muscular dystrophy, Parkinson's disease, phenylketonuria, spina bifida or hydrocephalus. Apply to your local Health Board.

Drugs and Medicines Refund Scheme

You may also qualify for some financial assistance if you are paying for regular medication above a certain designated sum. Apply to your local Health Board.

Dental and Optical Services

To qualify you must have sufficient social insurance contributions, or receive an Invalidity Pension or long-term Disability Benefit. If you have been entitled to these services at age 60, you and dependent spouse or partner retain this entitlement for life. You or your spouse may qualify on reaching age 66 so it is worth applying when you reach this age. Treatment is provided by private dentists and opticians/ ophthalmic surgeons.

For Dental Benefit obtain an application form from a dentist on the social welfare panel. For Optical Benefit application forms, apply to the *Treatment Section, Department of Social, Community and Family Affairs, Letterkenny, Co Donegal, Telephone 01-8748444 or 074-25566.*

Hearing Aids

To qualify you need to have a sufficient number of social insurance contributions, and if you qualify, your spouse does also. You can claim half the cost of a hearing aid, (up to a maximum sum). Apply to the *Department of Social, Community and Family Affairs, Letterkenny, Co Donegal, Telephone 01-8748444 or 074-25566.*

Aids and Appliances

To qualify you need to be able to show that the medical and surgical aids/appliances are part of your hospital treatment. Alternatively, the Health Board may contribute to the cost of buying an aid for you, or lend it to you if the need is short-term. Apply to your local Health Board.

The National Rehabilitation Board (NRB) has a Disability Resource Centre where aids and equipment suitable for people with a disability can be seen and tried out. Information is also available on costs and suppliers. Contact the *Disability Resource Centre, National Rehabilitation Board, 44 North Great Georges Street, Dublin 1, Telephone 01-8747503.*

Community Care Services

These services are organised and provided locally and can vary quite a bit from place to place. In some areas the services are provided by the Health Board, either directly or indirectly through voluntary organisations. Some communities services are provided almost totally through voluntary effort.

You can find out what services are available in your area by asking at your local health centre, or your Citizens Information Centre, at your GP surgery or at your local library.

The following is an A–Z of some of the services which may be available in your community

Chiropody Service

A limited chiropody service is provided by health boards. Apply to your local health centre.

Day Centres and Clubs

Some areas have day centres operated by the health board or a voluntary organisation. They overcome the isolation of people living alone and offer a respite for carers. Apply to your local health centre.

Day Hospitals

Nationally there are a small number of day hospitals (usually attached to hospitals) which offer out-patient services such as physiotherapy and occupational therapy. Apply to your local health centre.

Home Helps

Many health boards and voluntary organisations employ home helps to help people in their own homes with such chores as housework, meal preparation and shopping. If you can afford it, you may be asked to contribute to the cost. Apply to your local health centre.

Laundry Service

This may be provided by a local voluntary organisation. Apply to your local health centre.

Library Service

Public libraries are provided all over the country by the local authorities. Many have large-print books to facilitate people with poor sight. You may qualify for a block ticket which allows you to take out up to six books at a time and to hold on to them for three months without penalty. Libraries are a good source of local information, and may have daily papers and magazines for reading there. Some libraries organise special events for older people.

A Braille lending library and a talking book service (in which spoken versions of books are available on tape) is operated by the National Council for the Blind. The council also provides radio cassette players for blind people. Apply to the *National Council for the Blind, 45 Whitworth Road, Drumcondra, Dublin 9, Telephone 01-8307033.*

Meals on Wheels

This is the name applied to the service which provides and delivers a hot meal during the middle of the day to people not in a position to cook for themselves due to disability, illness or old age. The service may be a partnership between a health board, social service centre and local voluntary support. If you can afford it, you may be asked to contribute towards the cost of your meal. Apply to your local health centre.

Occupational Therapist

Most Health Boards employ occupational therapists. They can suggest and supply a number of aids and appliances to help with mobility or dexterity, they can also advise on adapting a house for a disabled person or for long-term convalescence. Apply to your local health centre.

Public Health Nurses

All Health Boards employ public health nurses who provide nursing services to people at home. Their services are normally free if you are aged 65 and over, and/or hold a medical card. Apply to your local health centre.

Respite Care

Respite care is provided at a number of locations round the country for people with different disabilities. The purpose is to give carers a break. A list of respite care facilities is available from the *National Rehabilitation Board, 25 Clyde Road, Dublin 4, Telephone 01-6684181.*

Social Workers

All health boards employ social workers who may be able to provide advice and support on problems or difficulties you may have. Apply to your local health centre. Most large hospitals also employ social workers who can discuss problems arising from an illness. Ask at the social work department of the hospital. Many voluntary organisations also employ social workers.

Appeal

If you have a problem with a health board service, entitlement, allowance or payment, you should write to the Chief Executive Officer of the Health Board.

Housing Issues

There are a number of grants, loans and services with the aim of improving the homes of older people.

Home Improvement Scheme

A special Task Force to improve the living conditions of elderly people living alone or in unfit accommodation was set up in 1992. The Task Force operates throughout the country in co-operation with the health boards, the ALONE organisation, St Vincent de Paul Society, and social services councils. The scheme is funded by the Department of the Environment and administered by local Health Boards. The work is carried out generally by FAS trainees. Where these are unavailable, local contractors may be used. Apply to the Community Care Section of your local Health Board.

House Improvement Grants for People with Disabilities

Special grants are available to improve the living accommodation of people with disabilities. A disability could include an elderly person with arthritis, who has suffered from a stroke, and is unable to walk upstairs.

Work which may qualify would include the provision of a downstairs bathroom or toilet, building of an extra room, providing ramps, widening door openings. The amount of the grant will vary from full to two-thirds of the cost of the work up to a maximum sum. You may receive technical advice from a community or hospital occupational therapist, or from the *National Rehabilitation Board, 25 Clyde Road, Dublin 4, Telephone 01-6684181*. Apply to the local authority before undertaking any work for which you want to claim a grant. See also Chapter 15 Growing Older – Some Hints for Carers.

Draught Proofing and Insulation

A free draught proofing and home insulation service is provided by non-profit organisations throughout the country to pensioners living alone. For further information contact *Energy Action, Unit 14, Newmarket Square, Dublin 8, Telephone 01-4545464*.

Special Concessions

A number of private firms and establishments offer special reductions to older people, and they tend to be offered as a concession rather than a right. Some concessions are available on production of a pension book. Others require only your travel pass.

In general, concessions may be available at cinemas, theatres, the National Concert Hall, the RDS, the Zoo. Discounted tickets or reductions may also be available at various sport fixtures country-wide such as GAA fixtures, horse racing, greyhound racing.

Some hairdressing establishments offer reductions to older people on certain days of the week. A number of dry cleaners give reductions on certain days. Some cablelink companies and DIY stores give concessions to older people.

Irish Ferries and Sealink give reductions on sea travel between Ireland and Britain to holders of a free travel pass. Under the Rail Europ scheme, people aged 60 and over may get reductions of up to 30% of the basic fares charged by railway and shipping companies in nearly all European countries. To avail of this scheme you should purchase a CTIC and RES card before you travel abroad. Such cards are available for a nominal sum from Iarnrod Eireann, Travel Centre, 35 Lower Abbey Street, Dublin 1, or through enquiry at mainline stations throughout the country. Golden Holidays for people aged 60 or over are available at a number of Irish hotels, farmhouses and resorts. Enquire at your local tourist information office.

Citizens Information Services

There are over 80 Citizen Information Centres round the country registered with the National Social Service Board. Information is provided on social welfare, health services, income tax, redundancy, housing, family law, consumer affairs and local organisations and services. CICs help people to get entitlements by helping them fill out forms and if necessary by contacting government agencies on their behalf. CICs also help people who are appealing against decisions. This service is free of charge for all.

The National Social Service Board, (NSSB) is a resource agency which aims to inform and empower individuals and communities by ensuring that they know their civil and social rights and entitlements, and the social services that exist to support them.

The NSSB brings together information on aspects of health, social welfare, taxation, housing and consumer affairs. It also provides information together with training to voluntary and statutory bodies which deal with individuals in need of information and advice. Contact the *National Social Service Board, Hume House, Dublin 4, Telephone 01-6059000.*

The Retirement Planning Council of Ireland also operate a free information, advice, and counselling service - pre or post retirement at Retirement Planning Council of Ireland, 27/29, Lower Pembroke Street, Dublin 2, Telephone 01-6613139, Fax 01-6611368.

Chapter 14

Willing and Able

"... to cause chaos by failure to make a will ..."

*C*on is a widower in his seventies and says he plans to be ∠
time. A pharmacist, he is enjoying life in retirement, surrou
loving family. He made his will many years ago, and updates it from
He says he hasn't a lot to leave, but that putting his affairs in order h∠
a feeling of peace and security. He has asked his children to choose what ∠
like from the family home, and has recorded each preferences in writing. "It ⌐ ∠ould
rows, not that there will be, everyone knows what the others have asked for, and there
has been no problem".

Advantages of Making a Will

While you can make a will at any time of your life over the age of 18, it is around middle-age that many people feel the need to put their affairs in order. Often, the sorting and tidying of documentation and assets that goes on before making a will can be very helpful, as well as the peace of mind and clarity gained from making decisions about your wishes.

Figures from the Probate Office in the Four Courts suggest that about a half of those who die in Ireland each year are intestate – they have not made a will. Wills are still a taboo subject. Many people don't want to consider the option, because it makes them confront their own – however distant – end. Some people just never get round to it, and others don't believe their bit of savings or capital merits such a legal move.

But, of course, you don't have to be the possessor of six Picassos and a turreted castle to cause chaos by a failure to leave a will. Ideally, do it when you're well, can think about it, and discuss it with family and friends if you wish.

There are four good reasons for making a will.

First, you ensure that your property passes to the people of your choice. Second you can choose the person whom you wish to look after your affairs after your death. This person is called the executor and their duties are quite important and extensive as you will see. You are free to appoint anyone you like, over 18 years old, though it may be advisable to get their agreement before such an appointment.

Thirdly, by making a will you may mitigate the incidence of inheritance tax to be paid. And fourth, you may avoid family rows.

If you don't make a will, your estate will be distributed and administered according to the 1965 Succession Act. You relinquish control. Unravelling your affairs will be more complicated for your family, the administration costs may be higher and the time taken to sort things out longer. Your assets are frozen till your affairs are put in order.

If you don't make a will and leave a spouse and no children, your spouse takes the entire estate. If you leave a spouse and children, your spouse will automatically get two-thirds of your estate and the remaining one third will be divided equally between your children. If your spouse has died before you, your children will inherit in equal shares. If you have neither spouse nor children, your parent(s) will inherit, and if they predecease you, your estate will be divided among brothers and sisters, or if you have none, among remoter relatives. If you have nobody belonging to you, the state is the ultimate beneficiary.

At first glance this may seem a fair way of disposing of your assets, but is it? You may have a handicapped child for whom you want to provide specially. You may be separated and have a second partner and family for whom you want to provide specially. You may want to favour an unmarried son or daughter who has lived in the family home and given you years of care. You may like to leave something to an old friend, or to a particular charity. Unless you state your wishes in legal terms, they cannot be known or honoured.

The Problems of Dying Intestate

Not making a will could cause unforeseen problems for your spouse. Legally, as we have said, s/he is entitled to two-thirds, and the children to one-third. But if the children want their share of their inheritance immediately, the family home may have to be sold to achieve this, and your spouse could technically be homeless. If you have a child under 16 or mentally handicapped child and fail to make a will, it is possible that someone would be appointed as guardian of your child that you would not consider suitable. So generally speaking, making a will gives much more scope for your wishes to be carried out as comprehensively as possible.

Separation and Divorce

One in 20 marriages in Ireland currently ends in separation or desertion. Most official figures agree that there are up 70,000–80,000 separated people in the country, who have the option of legally divorcing under the terms of divorce legislation which came into operation in 1997.

Under this legislation when a couple apply for divorce, the court will have to look at everything: maintenance, family property, children, tax, inheritances, pensions and so on – even if these have already been agreed under a deed of separation or decided by an earlier judicial separation court order.

What if you are legally separated or divorced and wish to make provision for your spouse and child in your will? A separation or divorce does not prohibit you from making provision for your family.

What if your marriage has legally ended and you do not wish to provide for your spouse and children? Whether or not you must provide for your spouse depends on your separation agreement or divorce decree. In agreements/decrees, a spouse agrees to a waiver of inheritance rights, and this is written into the deed of separation or divorce decree. In such cases, your spouse may not be entitled to anything on your death with a will. If there is no such waiver, s/he is entitled to a third of your estate, (or one half of your estate if you are childless). Legally, you cannot disinherit your children, and disinherited children may take a case under the Succession Act.

You may have a second family with a new partner to whom you are not married and want to provide for them under your will. Legally, no difference is made between marital and non-marital children, so your childrens' share of your estate will be divided equally among them all if you die without a will. How about providing financially for your partner? Again, if your spouse has agreed in writing to a waiver of inheritance rights, you will be able to provide financially for your partner. If no such waiver exists, your spouse can legally claim two thirds of your estate, with the remaining one-third going to your children – if there is no will – so your partner may benefit only indirectly through the children you may have had together.

What is the situation if you have obtained a divorce in a foreign jurisdiction and wish to provide for your spouse and family? Again, the childrens' rights are unaffected, and divorce does not change their rights. With regard to your spouse, it depends on whether the foreign divorce is recognised as valid. If so, then the position of your ex-spouse becomes that of your partner in the previous example. S/he has no legal rights to your property, as your current spouse will now be the major beneficiary. Notwithstanding a valid foreign divorce, a spouse can seek financial relief against the ex-spouse in certain circumstances if h/she does not remarry. This is also the case in an Irish divorce.

If the foreign divorce is not recognised by the Irish courts, (and many are not), then the inheritance rights remain with your first spouse who is deemed to be your lawful spouse in the eyes of the Irish jurisdiction.

If there is a valid divorce, (foreign or Irish), your ex-spouse can still have a claim to the estate, provided s/he has not remarried – but this claim may not be greater than that made if you were still legally married to each other.

The Value of Professional Advice

It is not advisable to attempt to draw up a will by yourself without the help and advice of a solicitor. A will is an important legal document. Home-made wills can go wrong. A solicitor can advise you how to carry out your wishes in a way that will give them effect. It's not good enough to say 'I leave the house to John and hope he'll take care of Mary'. You must be much more exact. Use simple language and be as precise as possible. Never use words like 'hope' or 'wish'. Be definite. A solicitor can also advise you to carry out your wishes in a way that is tax-efficient. For more information regarding tax and inheritances, see Chapter 5 – Reducing Your Tax Liability.

Wills must be in writing, signed by the testator, (person making the will) and witnessed by two people who cannot benefit. Generally speaking, wills once made remain permanently in force unless revoked or destroyed. A will becomes invalid on marriage, unless it was made in contemplation of the marriage.

It is possible that someone may be too ill to make a valid will. However, in the early stages of a degenerative disease, people may have the testamentary capacity to make a will. It may be necessary for a doctor to certify that someone is of sufficiently sound mind to make a will.

The Duties of an Executor

When you make your will, you may appoint whoever you wish as executor as we have said. The duties and powers of an executor are as follows:

- preserving, protecting and administering the estate properly, including insuring property, securing property
- maintaining a business as a going concern, if necessary.
- collecting all assets

- paying all debts
- notifying the surviving spouse of her/his legal rights as applicable
- obtaining a Grant of Probate
- obtaining all Tax Clearance Certificates including clearance from income tax
- obtaining clearance to distribute assets from the Department of Social Welfare
- Finally distributing the estate to all beneficiaries and obtaining the necessary receipts and indemnities from them.

(Although beneficiaries are primarily responsible for all tax due on inheritances, an executor is secondarily responsible, and consequently must satisfy her/himself that all taxes are paid before distributing the estate).

If you appoint the bank as executor it will charge a fixed rate based on a percentage of your total assets. This percentage varies from bank to bank, and generally speaking, appointing a bank as executor is an option only where there is a large estate.

Getting Your Affairs in Order

Try to simplify your estate as much as possible. If you have assets abroad which are of minimum value, it would be useful to bring them home to Ireland during your lifetime. The cost of doing so is negligible, and would save later on time and expense.

It's a good idea to list your assets – property, investments, insurance policies, stocks and shares. If you are leaving some property in trust for minors, or ill or handicapped relatives, you may appoint a trustee to oversee this. If you are leaving something to an invalid, make sure it does not interfere with her/his entitlements to state benefits. List your creditors also as they will have first call on your assets at death.

As well as listing your assets and liabilities for the purpose of making a will, it is useful to leave a list of assets accompanying, (not attached to) the will. This will be a good guide to your executor. Try to keep your papers safely in one place.

While spouses may make wills together, each is free to make a new will at any later stage. You cannot disinherit a spouse, unless s/he is guilty of certain crimes against you, or has deserted you for more than two years. A spouse can also be disinherited where certain orders have been made by the courts under the legislation governing judicial separation, divorce and family violence.

If children feel unfairly discriminated against under the terms of a will, they can apply to the court who will look at the case and will decide to make the sort of provision a prudent and just parent would do. The court also takes into account monies already given, educational costs, gifts. In this instance, the courts take a moral rather than a legal viewpoint.

Having Financial Affairs in Joint Names

Financial matters flow more smoothly for a married couple when bank accounts are in joint names. If a spouse dies, the account continues automatically in the name of the survivor. When accounts are not in joint names, the surviving un-named spouse will not be able to gain access to them until a Grant of Probate is granted by the court. If they need immediate money, they will have to raise an overdraft by way of an executor's account.

Probate is basically proof that a will is valid. Banks will not act on the basis of a will unless it has been admitted to probate. An executor may obtain a Grant of Probate from the Probate Office, Personal Applicants Section, The High Court, Four Courts, Dublin 7, Telephone 01-8725555. A solicitor's advice is recommended here, because of the extensive duties and liabilities of an executor. To obtain a Grant of Probate, you need to make a revenue return, file a Revenue Certificate in the Probate Office with the will. A simple Grant of Probate can take up to 12 weeks to obtain, but may be granted more quickly.

Similarly if the home is held in joint names as joint tenants, it automatically becomes the survivor's sole property on the spouse's death. Having the home changed from single to joint ownership is simply done, but you will need the services of a solicitor. Under the Family Home Protection Act, no stamp duty or registration fee is payable. Legal costs are normally modest, where the title is straightforward.

Don't think because you make a will you give up a right to your assets, you can use an asset all through your life, beneficiaries don't get rights in advance. You can still go on that world cruise. A will takes effect only on your death. You may change your will at any time, make new bequests, or do whatever you wish. Keep your will in an envelope, somewhere safe. Keep all the relevant documentation in one bundle with the will. Alternatively you can keep your will in the bank or with your solicitor. Let people close to you know where your will is located.

Example of a Brief but Valid Will

I (name) of (address) hereby revoke all former wills and codicils at any time heretofore made by me, and I declare this to be my last will. I give devise and bequeath all my property of whatsoever nature and kind to my spouse... and I appoint him (her) sole executor (executrix) of this my will. Dated this...(day) of... (month)... (year)

signed (name)

Signed by the testator as and for his last will in the presence of us both present at the same time who in his presence and in the presence of each other have hereunto subscribed our names as witnesses.

signed... (witnesses).

Remember witnesses should not be people who benefit under the will.

Powers of Attorney

Many people assume they can manage their affairs in old age by giving a relative power of attorney. This works if the relative is completely trustworthy. A power of attorney ceases effect when the person who gave the power dies. Under the Powers of Attorney Act 1996, a special type of powers of attorney, called an enduring power, continues in force even if the person who gave the power becomes unable to manage their affairs by reason of a disease of the mind.

Chapter 15

Growing Older –
Some Hints for Carers

Caring for relatives at home

*N*ora *now in her seventies spent forty years workin*,
*returning to the Co Kerry town where she was bo*ı

At the beginning, readjustment was difficult: "It's very diffe,
back on a holiday from when you come back to live. I expected th
*behind but it had gone, and it took me a long time to get used to t*ı

*She has suffered a number of heart attacks in the last few years. "*ℕ
*good the spirit is, it's difficult when the body lets you down. But throug*ı   *ss*
I have discovered good friends and neighbours and they are important to ı *c. I still*
enjoy life. I knit, I paint, I garden, I read. I grow plants".

Growing Older

While many people are living healthily and independently into old age,
a proportion become frail, ill, dependent and disabled. At some stage in your
life you may have whole or part responsibility for an elderly parent, or an
ill or disabled relative. In this chapter we discuss some aspects of such caring
– including caring for someone at home, room conversion for disability, and
nursing home care. See also Chapter 6 - Knowing Your Entitlements.

Caring for a Relative at Home

Should you become a carer either full-time or part-time, you join an
estimated band of 100,000 people. Caring can cover anything from
dropping in to see an elderly parent every day on your way home from
work, to something full time, strenuous and fairly exhausting.

A national survey indicates that one in three people being looked after
by a carer is housebound, and about one in seven is confined to bed.
Typically, they can no longer prepare or cook a meal for themselves, and
may need help with dressing, washing or bathing.

The difficulties may be more than physical. Memory loss, angry
outbursts, mood swings, confusion, depression and sleeplessness can affect a
minority of elderly people being cared for on a regular basis. One in four
suffer these symptoms occasionally.

If you become a family carer, you should know that the job can impose
a variety of stresses and strains, both financial and emotional. One in three
carers experiences financial strain as a result of giving up work, and through
the extra costs incurred in caring.

what can help? A carer's allowance was introduced in the late 1980s. But only a small minority of carers currently claim it due to stringent means testing. To find out if you do qualify, contact the Carers Allowance Section, Pensions Services Office, College Road, Sligo, Telephone 01-8748444/071-69800.

In some families there are members who pull their weight more than others. If you find yourself landed with all or most of the decisions and responsibilities of an elderly parent, it may be time to call in other family members to discuss how the burden could be shared more equally. Some households draw up rota systems where grown up sons and daughters take their turn at the minding. Older grandchildren can also become involved. In families where one member is the major carer, other family members can offer support by visiting regularly, and provide day, weekend or holiday cover so that the carer can have some time off.

So it would be important to try to take care of your own needs while looking after someone else. The Carer's Association was set up to offer this type of support. From its contact with carers, the association lists their needs as social and moral support, financial help, information and advice, respite care, more nursing aids, practical help and training with tasks such as lifting and bathing, access to back up services, and counselling services.

The association has attempted to respond to those needs by offering advice and information to carers, by the setting up of carers self-help groups and by holding information evenings. The association also runs a Respite Homecare Programme to give carers a break. The programme provides a respite worker to go into the family home to give practical help with bathing, lifting and personal care, spending 2 - 8 hours a day depending on the need. This allows the carer take a rest, look after other work, go shopping, have some time to themselves, meet friends. With more funding, the Carer's Association could expand and develop this much-needed programme.

More information and support on all aspects of caring is available from the *Carer's Association, St Mary's Community Centre, Richmond Hill, Dublin 6, Telephone 01-4974498.*

Home Adaptations for Illness or Age

The Disability Federation of Ireland reckon that every year many thousands of homes need adaptation to cope with sudden illness, disability or the effects of frail old age.

Grants for home adaptation are given by the Department of Environment. A grant may be available where an extra room or other structural changes are necessary such as a ramp, wider doorways or an internal lift.

If you are a homeowner, the amount of the grant is up to a maximum of £8,000 or two thirds of the cost, whichever is lower. If you live in a local authority house or flat, you may be granted the full cost of conversion. For more information, contact the Department of Environment, Custom House, Dublin 1, Telephone 01-6793377, or your local authority.

There are usually three options - convert a room, either upstairs or downstairs into an extra shower room or an ensuite bed/sitting room, convert the garage, or build on an extension at the side or more typically out the back. The chosen option will depend on house size, layout and family preference. Some older people are nervous about sleeping downstairs, others may feel cut off upstairs - it's a personal choice.

Planning permission is not required for internal work, nor for converting a garage or building a rere extension of 23 square metres or less, (providing there has been no prior extension which would mean the new work extends the original flooring by over 23 metres).

A common adaptation is to build a ground floor shower room toilet and wash basin. If for a wheelchair user, the room should measure at least 9' x 6' to allow sufficient room for shower, wheelchair and carer, if necessary.

Many special features can be included. A toilet may be higher than normal. Lever taps are easier to use than conventional types, rocker lights are easier than switches. The shower may have a hinged or movable seat, the water temperature should be thermostatically controlled and the unit could have a vertically sliding nozzle that can be levelled at different body parts and heights. There should be grab rails. The cost of designing and building a shower room would be approximately £8,000 - 9,000 plus VAT.

If a wheelchair is needed, a new or converted bed/sitting room should be at least 13' x 10', large enough for bed, chair, television, book case, for a wheelchair to turn, and for the door to be opened or closed easily. Electric sockets should be at waist, rather than floor level.

There are two types of lifts available. A lift that goes up and down a rail on the side of the staircase will cost approximately £3,500 to buy and from £2,000 to install. If the stairs are not so accommodating, it may be possible to install a lift which rises vertically from living room to bedroom. This lift can cost from £7,500. (From £10,000 fitted).

Providing access in and out of the house may also be necessary. A simple concrete ramp with rail can cost from £500, but, depending on proportional height of house to garden, a more complicated ramp or step combination could cost up to £1,800 or even more.

You shouldn't go ahead with an extension or adaptation without first being granted approval by the local authority. It is important to retain a professional who understands the design and logistical implications of disability. Your health board or community occupational therapist may recommend some suitable names to you.

One occupational therapist offers the following advice on layout and design. Householders, she says, often don't think sufficiently long-term when considering building a granny flat or a home adaptation. The features which present no problem to the mobile, independent older person can cause difficulty as the years go by. Floor levels between rooms should be kept level, if necessary by removing door thresholds. When designing, it's important to project into the future.

Other short-term features are putting in a bath rather than a shower, building too narrow doors, and placing windows too high. Older people tend to spend some part of the day sitting down and it's frustrating if a view is inaccessible because windows are not set sufficiently low.

You should plan the conversion with maximum consultation with the older person regarding decor and design. All furniture should be strong and secure as some older people 'furniture crawl' - hold on to different items for support as they walk. If the piece is too flimsy, it might come down on top of them or cause them to fall.

The best type of chair for an older person is a stable, firm, high chair with arms. Avoid rockers, swivel chairs and low deep sofas which are difficult to stand up from. Rugs and mats should be tacked down to prevent tripping.

Know about adaptive equipment available for older people. These include non-skid materials in bath or shower, a kitchen trolley to transport items between surfaces when preparing a meal, telephone options such as light-up dial, large numbers and speakers, special kettles, trays, and tap turners. Install smoke detectors.

When arranging the room, store frequently used items - such as toiletries, clothing, shoes, dishes, foodstuffs and cooking utensils - close to waist height.

The bed should not be too low in height and should have a firm rather than a too soft mattress. A duvet will make bed-making easier. Choose an electric over-blanket rather than an under-blanket, as incontinence could create problems with the latter type. Over-blankets are safer too, if you forget to turn them off. Place a telephone at the bedside with emergency numbers in large print. Install a lamp or light at the bed. Have a bell or buzzer near the older person at night.

A home care team may be available locally to help you during a crisis. This team includes a physiotherapist, occupational therapist, care attendant who collectively help with bathing, dressing, offer advice on social welfare entitlements, mobility aids. The physiotherapist can offer exercises to improve mobility. Apply to your local health centre.

Caring at a Distance

You may have an elderly parent who lives alone or with a spouse and manages quite well but needs some support from family and community services outlined above.

Reach Out Campaign

Don't underestimate the value of good neighbours. If your relative has lived in the same place for many years, s/he may have built up firm local friendships. Good neighbours can help you keep in touch if you are not able to visit every day. Dublin Corporation's 'Reach Out – Be a Good Neighbour' campaign builds on this local network of goodwill and has been extended to other corporations throughout the country. Basically, it asks people to be aware of elderly neighbours living alone nearby. You can do this by keeping an eye on them, drop in from time to time. Be tactful and do not impose where you may not be needed, but bear in mind that those who appear to have no friends and who reject help may be at greatest risk.

Hypothermia

Hypothermia is a silent killer which claims some elderly victims every winter. The name refers to the state when the body is unable to maintain a normal temperature of 98.4 degrees F and the body temperature drops dangerously low. Normally, when we feel cold, we put on more clothes, warm the room, have a hot drink or take some exercise.

Older people may get to a stage where they are too confused or unfit to take action when they are cold. Also an old person does not retain bodily heat as efficiently as someone younger, and may not be so resilient. Certain drugs and illnesses actually lower body temperature. The state of hypothermia may pass unnoticed. Even when an older person's temperature is taken, people may not be alerted, as the standard thermometer is registered only down to 95 degrees F.

Danger signs you need to look out for are loss of appetite, drowsiness, swollen and pale skin and mental confusion. The body feels cold to the touch, the breathing shallow and slow. In suspected hypothermia, the skin should be felt under the clothing. If it feels cold, hypothermia is almost certain.

The temperature in homes in which old people live should be maintained at over 60 degrees F. Loose layers of clothing help to trap the heat rather like a thermos flask effect. Shawls, stoles, knee rugs will help, as will wearing a hat as 20% of body heat is lost through the head.

During Winter or in cold weather an old person should have at least one warm room, (with temperature at about 65 degrees F) where they spend most of the day. It is important to visit more frequently in winter. If heating is by coal, sufficient fuel should be available and there should be a fire guard. Central heating systems should be controlled, and any electrical or gas fires should be safe in use and in situation.

Mild hypothermia when people are still conscious can be treated with warm drinks, and by wrapping in a blanket and by heating the room. If you suspect hypothermia, call the GP. While waiting, don't try to warm the person too quickly with a hot water bottle, or by rubbing the skin briskly. This could kill by causing the blood to rush to the surface of the skin and away from heart and brain. Don't pile with too heavy blankets. Severe hypothermia must be treated in hospital.

Nursing Homes

The day may come when you have to make the decision that your elderly or incapacitated family member needs nursing home care. Under The Health (Nursing Homes) 1990 Act which became law in 1993, nursing homes must comply with regulations involving patient care and welfare, staff ratios and training, safety and general standards before being approved and registered by the health board.

Nursing home staffs agree that many families place an elderly relative in care reluctantly: "Families usually feel very guilty when they contact us. They feel as if they have failed the person, though often they are at the end of their tether and there comes a time when they can no longer manage", says one matron.

When choosing a nursing home, get a list of approved homes from the health board. Visit a number. Be sensitive to atmosphere. A good place will feel warm and welcoming. Ask questions, talk to other residents, talk about your relative. It is a good idea to visit both with and without an appointment.

Surprising discrepancies can be noted between the two occasions.

Alarm bells should ring if a place is unkempt and untidy, or it looks glamorous, but is cold and unhomely. Trust your feelings. Most nursing homes now try to offer a programme of activities for residents. There should be access to daily papers radio and television, and local library service. Card games may be organised, many nursing homes now provide reminiscence therapy, art and craft classes.

How to Choose a Nursing Home

- if possible, discuss the decision with the person concerned
- discuss the decision with family, GP, public health nurse
- identify your relative's medical, physical and social needs
  e.g. continence care, dietary requirements, mobility, medication
- think about accessibility to facilitate regular visiting
- contact the health board and check that the homes you are considering are approved and registered
- make a short list of suitable homes
- make an appointment to visit each
- write a list of the questions you wish to ask
- if possible ensure that the person concerned should visit the proposed home(s) also
- check what is covered in the stated charges. There may be extra costs for laundry, for instance.
- remember that private nursing home costs may be eligible for tax relief

What to Look Out for When You Visit

- is the atmosphere cheerful and friendly?

- does the home seem like a comfortable and pleasant place to live?

- are the staff friendly and informative?

- are residents treated with courtesy and respect. For example, are their food preferences considered?

- may residents bring possessions with them such as small items of furniture, pictures, ornaments?

- are regular activities planned and may they continue their own hobbies and interests?

- does the home provide regular occupational therapy and physiotherapy sessions?

- are visiting times flexible?

- how welcome are you made as a family unit?

- do residents have a say in how the home is run? Is there a residents' committee?

If you are paying for a relative to be cared for in an approved nursing home, you may be entitled to a subvention from the local authority.

Chapter 16

The Potential
of Grey Power

Grey power

M *ichael wakes up at six o'clock in the morning ready for action. A postman for 45 years, his body clock is still conditioned to an early start: "My round was about six miles, I did some of it by bike but mainly I walked, it was a lot of miles over the years. When I started there were three deliveries, and we worked six days a week. Now it's only one delivery, and a five day week.*

He has lived 47 years on the same street, "I was born, bread and buttered here. The city has changed so much, but we still have good neighbours and a good sense of community spirit.

"I had to retire, I didn't have a choice, a pity really, I think I have a few more miles in me yet. I wasn't really looking forward to retirement, and I haven't kept in touch with people at work. Someone said to me when you go outside the gate, don't bother coming back, because they will have forgotten about you. But I have planned a once a year reunion with some old friends from the job, and we hope to keep that up".

The Sleeping Giant

At the beginning of this century one in every 25 Europeans was aged over 60. By the year 2020 older people will be one in four, by 2030, one in three. More people are living longer. This has implications for every facet of life - work, retirement, social services, education, housing, leisure, politics and rural life.

Today growing numbers of older people are active, interested in issues and have some time on their hands, in other words, a significant voting force. It would be a foolish politician who neglects one voter in four, or one voter in three. However, at present only a minority of older Irish people are actively involved in campaigning or seem to realise the potential of their clout.

Grey Power

Other countries are more aware. Nobody believed America would grow old gracefully. And far from fading away, as yesterday's middle-aged generation moved on, they celebrated the rite of passage by founding the powerful American Association of Retired Persons, (AARP) and the Grey Panther movement. In Europe pensioners have also taken to the streets with slogans and placards to lobby as a group for their rights.

In this chapter we look at some of the issues facing older people as individuals and as a group and review some of the positive action being taken.

Job Discrimination

Economic pressure to reduce the workforce has resulted in discrimination against older workers whose numbers are steadily declining. A major Eurolink Age survey found that:

- increasing numbers of the over 50s are obliged to retire early regardless of ability or health
- older workers are excluded from retraining or promotion
- age discrimination in recruitment policies starts from age 40 in most countries.

The survey recommended that public authorities should act to outlaw age discrimination – in recruitment advertisements, training and employment promotion measures and involuntary early retirement.

Would anti-discrimination legislation help the present trend? While laws do not immediately change attitudes, legislation may be applied in the courts, raise awareness of the injustice of age discrimination, and give expression to what society expects. The 1996 Employment Equality Bill is seeking to make discrimination in Irish employment illegal on the grounds of age.

It's also worth noting that by 2005 one worker in two will be over 40. With fewer young people in the workforce the skills and experience of older workers will become more valuable. Some years ago when opening a new branch, the British DIY chainstore B & Q stated that all applicants had to be over 50 years of age. The experiment has paid off in that the branch exceeded its staff sales target by 40%, the biggest increase in any of the company's outlets, staff turnover has been less and absentee levels lower than other branches.

Rural Life

One in four of older people in Europe lives in a rural area. One in two farmers are aged over 55, and some studies have identified sole elderly rural women as a particularly vulnerable group.

But in spite of their numbers, the needs, desires and living conditions of older rural people are not always taken into account by planning authorities. Rural communities suffer from a declining agricultural sector, poor infrastructure, depopulation and comparatively inadequate services. In many communities the village shop, post office, school, banks, and petrol station have closed. Irish research has identified the lack of accessible public transport in rural areas as a main area of concern for older people.

There are some innovative schemes to counter this. Forum, North West Connemara Rural Project illustrates how community development projects can lessen rural isolation. Its projects include establishing a daily transport service between Galway and North Connemara and setting up five resources centres used by older people for socialising, hairdressing and chiropody. *Forum, Letterfrack, Connemara, Co Galway, Telephone 095-41116.*

Living Arrangements

Too often the only answers offered to the housing needs of frail older people are residential care and sheltered housing. But effective housing polices need to take into account the complexity and diversity of personal needs, social networks and life-styles. In response to the expressed wish of most older people, it is now felt that schemes which enable them to live on in their own homes should remain the focus of policy and research.

In surveys most older people cite having friendly neighbours in their vicinity as absolutely necessary to their independence and well-being. This should give food for thought to service providers. A relatively small input of resources to buttress the informal support of family and neighbours may prevent having to deploy much greater resources if people are left to cope and find the burden too great.

In Clonubur, Co Galway, a convent has been converted into a health and day centre. Bungalows for local older people whose homes had become run down have been built next door to the centre. Managed by North Connemara Voluntary Housing Association, the project shows how existing resources can be utilised through collaborative local effort.

Ageism

Underlying many discriminatory policies towards older people is the issue of ageism. Ageism shows itself in what people say and do in referring to older people. It shows itself in seeing an older person as part of a group, 'the elderly', 'the aged', rather than an individual. And often the group is seen as predominately needing care, attention and generally being a burden.

'If age discrimination was entirely a matter of individual attitudes, it could be more easily tackled. It is when ageist attitudes become part of the rules of institutions, govern the conduct of social life and blend imperceptibly into everyday values and attitudes that they have a drastic effect on the way older people live their lives'. *'Age - the Unrecognised Discrimination'* Age Concern.

So ageism is a kind of institutionalised discrimination. As well as some of the discriminatory areas already discussed, it can include more expensive car insurance for older people, restricted insurance cover, being pushed to the back of the medical queue, under-representation in public media in proportion to numbers. Women are often hit hardest in a combination of ageism and sexism. As women age, they tend to disappear from television screens as newsreaders and presenters and from front of house staff in office reception areas.

Why is society ageist? Research indicates that at a profound level we have negative attitudes before we fear old age. Portraying older people as different and marginalised helps to distance us from what we fear in our own future.

Good Reasons to Change

Many people are now coming to see that ageism harms us all. It's damaging to you as an older person if you are made feel worthless and lacking in value. It's damaging to society as a whole if a section of the community is under-represented.

Allowing young people to hold a skewed or lop-sided view of old age is selling them short too. Seeing older people as burden rather than resource powerfully reinforces fears and terrors about old age among society as a whole, thus creating a self-fulfiling prophecy.

So one of the challenges in growing older is to bridge the information gap between perception and reality - in Ireland as elsewhere. Changing ageist attitudes must involve more older people themselves telling it like it is.

Another reason to challenge the stereotype is that of sheer weight of numbers. The number and proportion of older people in the Irish population are expected to continue rising over the next thirty years. This is a new issue for society to deal with. In 1900 the life expectancy for a man was 60, a woman 67. Today if you are a 60 year old man, on average, you can expect to live for another 17 years. If you are a 60 year old woman, you can expect to live another 21 years. By the year 2011, a sixty year old man will expect to live another 19 years and a 60 year old woman another 23 years. Never before in the history of humankind have so many of us lived so long. Or so hopefully. Taking a new look at the life trajectories of older people shows not an inevitable downward curve, but a flow that stops, shifts, rests, then leaps ahead again. The traditional long-accepted vision of age as decline may be due to the fact that many of the studies were carried out on elderly people living in institutions without resources and family contacts.

The Irish Congress of Trade Unions and the National Federation of Pensioners' Associations have drawn up a Charter of Rights for the Elderly. It includes the following:

- the right to live independent active and full lives without discrimination on grounds of age
- the right to an adequate income in retirement
- the right to suitable living accommodation. A range of housing should be available to include sheltered housing, purpose built flats, voluntary housing associations and controlled rented accommodation.
- the right to a proper nursing home service if frail and physically incapacitated.
- the right to hospitalisation, medical services and proper community health services
- the right to participate in formal and informal adult education
- the right to pre-retirement facilities to include paid time off to attend retirement planning courses
- the right to participate in and be represented on appropriate bodies dealing with matters concerning the elderly
- the right to protection against violence
- the right to travel and recreational facilities providing opportunities for personal expression, development and fulfilment.

New Consumer Challenges

The age bulge of large numbers of competent older people is a consumer challenge. A revolution led by older shoppers is set to transform retailing in the year 2000 and beyond. It will involve a rethink of attitudes towards you as an older consumer to ensure that your spending power, rights, choices and access are recognised.

Already some advertisers are developing new stereotypes. Universities are actively courting more mature students. The holiday trade is shifting away from Club 18-30 as the only travel model. Architects, town planners, industrial designers will need to ensure that their services and strategies cater for the changing and ageing face of Ireland.

Grey power is a marketing opportunity for many. As an older shopper, you have more financial muscle than ever before. You are active, affluent and have a disposable income to spend.

The age bulge has implications for the development of new ranges of products, and the adaptation of many existing ones. Much of the country's facilities are designed for young people, and as green turns to grey, so goods and services will similarly have to change. This would mean for example, more large print books and magazines, more accessible packaging of many consumer goods, and a growing market for home and garden products such as light weight wheelbarrows, spring loaded spades and electric strimmers to replace backbreaking edging sheers.

An older population has implications for customer care in other ways. There may be an increase in mail order shopping, giving choice to immobile or housebound people.

Who's Campaigning

Older people's organisations include those run by older people themselves and those raising awareness of older people's issues and/or welfare with the emphasis on autonomy and self–help. Some are single issue groups, others have a wider brief.

Age and Opportunity

Age & Opportunity is a national non–governmental organisation which aims to promote positive attitudes to ageing, The organisation has examined the nature and extent of ageist policies, highlights age discrimination, promotes the creative and artistic talents of older people and challenges inaccurate ageist stereotyping. Age & Opportunity co–ordinates a variety of projects each year at international, national and local level, and also organises workshops, training courses, seminars and conferences. Age & Opportunity offers a library and information resources unit, and may be contacted by groups or individuals. *Age & Opportunity, The Marino Institute of Education, Griffith Avenue, Dublin 9, Telephone 01-8530443.*

Age Action Ireland

Age Action Ireland is a national non–governmental organisation representing a network of organisations providing services for older people, and working as a development agency promoting better services and policies for older people. Age Action offer an information/library service, publishes a monthly bulletin and a directory of services for older people in Ireland, organises national and regional conferences, seminars and training programmes. *Age Action Ireland, 114-116 Pearse Street, Dublin 2, Telephone 01-6779892*

Age Alliance Ireland

Age Alliance Ireland, a lobby group, has established a transport action committee which brings together representatives of older people, people with disabilities and parents of young children all of whom suffer from the lack of safe, accessible public transport. *Age Alliance, ℅ Age & Opportunity, The Marino Institute of Education, Griffith Avenue, Dublin 9. Telephone 01-8530443.*

Federation of Active Retirement Association

Federation of Active Retirement Associations, (FARA), referred to in other chapters, has enhanced the lives of thousands of retired people all over the country. While not necessarily a campaigning group, FARA offers a positive model of post-work life, and demonstrates the value and resource of older people. FARA is an umbrella body for the network of active retirement associations round the country which run educational, cultural and sporting activities. *FARA, 59-61 Dame Street, Dublin 2, 01-6792142.*

Grand Parents Obliterated

Grand Parents Obliterated (GPO) is a support and a campaigning group, representing grandparents who are denied contact with their grandchildren due to marital separation. In almost all cases, the lost grandchildren are the children of a son rather than a daughter. Grand Parents Obliterated want a change in the Guardianship of Infants Act to include grandparents as suitable guardians under certain circumstances. They also want improved access. At present, there is provision for a son to apply for access for grandparents in cases where this is denied. *Grand Parents Obliterated, 29 Kildare Road, Dublin 12.*

Irish Association of Older People

Irish Association of Older People is a voluntary organisation which aims to be a voice for people aged 55 and over, to represent their interests, campaign on their behalf and to help create an environment in which the value and capacity of older people will be seen and heard in the community. *Irish Association of Older People, Room GO2, University College, Earlsfort Terrace, Dublin 2, Telephone 01-4750013.*

Irish Senior Citizens National Parliament

Irish Senior Citizens National Parliament was set up in November 1996 to represent the interests of older people. The parliament meets monthly to debate relevant issues and makes submissions to government. Elected parliament members are now representing a growing network of 'constituents' round the country. *Irish Senior Citizens National Parliament, 32 Parnell Square, Dublin 1, Telephone 01-8782541.*

National Council for the Elderly

National Council for the Elderly is an advisory body to the Minister for Health on all aspects of ageing and the welfare of elderly people. It publishes reports based on research which are of particular interest to policy-makers and those concerned with older people's issues. These include rural Ireland, nursing home provision, attitudes to older people, social services. A list of publications is available from the Council. *National Council on Aging and Older People, 22 Clanwilliam Street, Dublin 2, Telephone 01-6766484.*

National Federation of Pensioners Associations

National Federation of Pensioners Associations is an umbrella group for pensioners associations throughout Ireland which aims to protect and promote the interests of pensioners. *National Federation of Pensioners Associations, c/o Irish Congress of Trade Unions, 31 Parnell Square, Dublin 1, Telephone 01-6680641.*

Older Women's Network

Older Women's Network (OWN) promotes the sharing of knowledge, skills and experiences of older women across Europe in order to challenge negative stereotypes of age, gender, race, disability and sexuality and to promote the rights of older women. Ireland, through Age & Opportunity is a founding member. *OWN, c/o Age & Opportunity, The Marino Institute of Education, Griffith Avenue, Dublin 9, 01-8370570.*

And last but not least...

Retirement Planning Council of Ireland

Retirement Planning Council of Ireland (RPCI) sets out to create awareness of the problems of retirement, offers information, develops and organises preparation for retirement courses, promotes research into retirement planning. The Council works constantly to establish ways to allow the energies, skills, knowledge and experience of retired people to be used for their own good and that of the community.

The Council includes both corporate and individual members, and welcomes membership enquiries. Membership entitles you to attend the Council's annual conference and annual general meeting, receive a regular newsletter and to avail of the Council's information and advice service on all aspects of retirement.

The Council offers in-company retirement preparation courses, open courses, retirement modules or complete courses for individual companies, and early retirement courses. The Council publishes a regular newsletter offering information and promoting discussion on relevant retirement topics. The newsletter is of interest to pensioners, employees, employers, trade unions, health officials, government, voluntary organisations. A Volunteer Service which supports retired people looking for some voluntary work operates under the Council's umbrella.

Retirement Planning Council of Ireland, Retirement Consultants, 27/29 Pembroke Street Lower, Dublin 2, Telephone 01-6613139.

A Final Word

A Final Word on Retirement from the Retirement Planning Council

The Retirement Planning Council of Ireland have been working with people, helping them to plan for their retirement for more than two decades. We have noticed many changes in that time, so what is the current experience?

Most certainly less than a decade ago it was not uncommon for many people to view retirement in negative terms. 'Life without work for many appeared like the end of the world'. Our experience now is that the vast majority of people recognise retirement for what it can be, namely, *a time of opportunity not threat*.

Initially it might appear that your options are limited and choices restricted, but hopefully this book has helped to identify many new possibilities and opportunities for you to have a long and rewarding retirement. It has deliberately focused on the areas that we find provide the greatest reward for people in a well planned retirement. Any time and effort spent in planning for changes in the areas of Time, Health, Money, and Relationships, will be time well spent. Refer to the chapters in this book dealing with these key areas regularly to ensure you are on the right track.

If you are one of those people for whom retirement still appears to be a threat, we hope you find comfort and solace in this book, and that it gives you the strength and hope to strive to achieve the most you can from your retirement. There are very many organisations listed in the chapters of this book, whose work is dedicated to helping you make this period of your life enjoyable. Don't be afraid to contact them and avail of their expertise.

Our final word is to recognise and realise the opportunity of retirement and thereby diminish the fears, by looking back with pride on your achievements, and let go of those things you cannot change, as they will surely imprison you. Look forward to what is potentially a most rewarding period of your life and think of what Charles F. Kettering said *" My interest is in the future because I am going to spend the rest of my life there."*

The richness of years – of experience,

love and pain – are locked

inside every old person

And as more people survive

to old age so the world grows richer

To touch the old is to unlock the accumulated

wealth of years'.

Anon